Accreditation

Accreditation

A STRUGGLE OVER STANDARDS IN HIGHER EDUCATION

By WILLIAM K. SELDEN

Harper & Brothers
Publishers, New York

ACCREDITATION: A Struggle Over Standards in Higher Education

Do not laugh—

Do not weep,

Try to understand.

—ATTRIBUTED TO SPINOZA

Contents

vii

Preface

EDUCATORS from foreign countries, with whom I have had the pleasure of speaking on many occasions in the past several years, were the first to impress on me the need for a comprehensively written, non-detailed explanation of accrediting. Previously, A. Hollis Edens, President of Duke University; Reuben G. Gustavson, President of Resources for the Future; David D. Henry, President of the University of Illinois; and Albert N. Jorgensen, President of the University of Connecticut—each at one time president of the National Commission on Accrediting—as well as Arthur S. Adams, President of the American Council on Education, and Theodore A. Distler, Executive Director of the Association of American Colleges, had individually urged me to make an extensive study of this educational activity, in a field where there has been considerable misunderstanding and confusion. Then, at a meeting in the spring of 1958, a small group of medical doctors, doctors of veterinary medicine, dentists, and pharmacists, all actively engaged in accrediting, encouraged me to undertake the enjoyable and tantalizing task of writing this story of accreditation.

By coincidence, the theme—a struggle over standards in higher education—was developed as a result of the response to two talks which I gave in June 1958, one at The Catholic University of America and the other at the University of California in Los Angeles. Additional encouragement from those who read these speeches when they were printed led me ultimately to realize that accrediting is a manifestation in higher education of our form of civil government and political control. Just as there is struggle for control and influence in civil government, so there is struggle for control and influence of academic standards in higher education. And accreditation provides the focus for this latter struggle.

The material included in this monograph was selected after frequent discussions of accrediting with friends who must have despaired of my ever again conversing with enthusiasm on any other topic. My wife and my office associate, Mrs. Barbara Pope, not only have been long suffering in this respect but they have typed and re-read the manuscript for what to them must have seemed countless times. I am indebted to them for their helpful suggestions, for their many kindnesses, and for their encouragement.

Gray C. Boyce, Chairman of the Department of History, Northwestern University, W. H. Cowley, Professor of Higher Education, Stanford University, and William G. Land, Research Consultant in Education, Washington, D. C., have been unselfishly generous with comments and recommendations which have helped to improve the presentation.

I am also indebted to various members of the Executive Committee of the National Commission on Accrediting for suggestions which they have made, as well as to W. Earl Armstrong, Director, National Council for Accreditation of

Teacher Education; Lloyd E. Blauch, recently United States Assistant Commissioner for Higher Education; John S. Brubacher, Professor of the History and Philosophy of Education, Yale University; Edwin D. Duryea, Jr., Dean of Evening Division, Hofstra College; Ruth E. Eckert, Professor of Higher Education, University of Minnesota; Elmer Ellis, President, University of Missouri; John G. Hervey, Advisor, Council of Legal Education and Admissions to the Bar, American Bar Association; Raymond F. Howes, Staff Associate, American Council on Education; Carl W. McIntosh, Jr., President, Idaho State College; Carroll V. Newsom, President, New York University; Ernest T. Stewart, Executive Director, American Alumni Council; Ordway Tead, Vice President, Harper and Brothers; Edward L. Turner, recently Secretary, Council on Medical Education and Hospitals, American Medical Association; Elmer D. West, Director, Office of Statistical Information and Research; and F. L. Wormald, Associate Director, Association of American Colleges.

Carlos H. Baker, Professor of English, Princeton University, kindly consented to my borrowing his characters from *A Friend in Power* for the prologue and the epilogue.

William K. Selden

Washington, D. C.
July 1959

Prologue

To THE fictitious Edward Tyler it came as a shock, and a profound shock at that, when he was informed of his election to the presidency of the imaginary Enfield University.[1] It is true that for some time he had been a member of the faculty, as well as chairman of a department. But as a member of the faculty Committee of Six selected to advise the trustees in their choice of a president, he had never once considered himself a possible candidate. He had not even seriously daydreamed about the presidency. Instead, his personal thoughts for the future were concentrated upon his forthcoming sabbatical year in Europe on a Guggenheim fellowship.

As Chairman of the Department of Modern Languages, Tyler had not been unduly distracted by administrative responsibilities. Homer Vaughn, retiring after thirty years, had

[1] Baker (15).

served the institution well as its chief administrative officer. Never smitten with the thrill of teaching or of academic research, Vaughn had taken readily to the responsibilities of the presidency or, as it has been called, the "happy chaos." [2] A widower for some years, he could afford to devote endless hours to the details of administration, serving at the same time as "the representative of the general interest, attempting to reconcile the differences of specialists, whether they be subject-matter specialists or staff or administrative specialists." [3] One of Vaughn's successful accomplishments had been to save the faculty from the responsibility of administrative decisions and to allow them full freedom in their teaching and academic pursuits.

In this university atmosphere, Edward Tyler had pursued his primary academic interest—the life and writings of Voltaire—as enthusiastically if not as assiduously as he had when he was writing his doctoral dissertation. Voltaire was the reason for Tyler's projected trip to Europe, and Voltaire had absorbed his interests and his enthusiasms—until that sunny, warm day in June when the Board of Trustees changed his entire life and made him an administrator.

Commencement is always a time of intense activity on any campus. The announcement of a new president following a thirty year incumbency made this commencement season at Enfield University even more memorable through sustained excitement. The end of June, with President Vaughn's departure, had arrived before Tyler could begin to develop the institution-wide perspective necessary to meet his new responsibilities. Like "most faculty members, trained as specialists in their own particular field," he was "not well informed of the history of educational ideas." [4]

One of the first major issues confronting President Tyler was presented in a letter from a national professional as-

[2] Abbott (1), p. 65. [3] *Ibid.*, p. 62. [4] Cowley (64), p. 100.

sociation indicating that the accreditation of Enfield University would be in jeopardy unless certain improvements were made in the facilities provided for this professional division at the university. Agitated by what he considered to be the impertinence of any outside organization in dictating how a university should be operated, Tyler re-read the communication and perceived some further implications as to the incompetence of certain members of the Enfield faculty in this area of study. His immediate inclination was to dictate a reply of irritation over such proceedings, condemning outsiders for attempting to interfere with the rightful authority of colleges and universities to conduct their own affairs and make their own appointments as deemed appropriate.

Fortunately, at this point Tyler recalled a quotation from Voltaire:

> It is said that God is always on the
> side of the heaviest battalions.[5]

Before mounting an attack, President Tyler decided to learn more about accreditation and to find out which side did have the "heaviest battalions."

The study which he pursued proved to be most enlightening. From it he ascertained that accreditation is a method for controlling academic standards, and that as a result of a singular combination of social forces, this method has been developed in the United States in marked contrast to the systems employed in all other countries of the world.

[5] Letter to M. le Riche, February 6, 1770.

Accreditation

ONE

Not One But Seven Devils

OF THE hundreds and hundreds of volumes written about higher education in the United States it is surprising to note that no more than passing reference, if any at all, is made to accrediting, accreditation, or accreditment, as it is variously called. This lack of attention is incongruous when one appreciates how extensively accrediting has influenced the development of higher education in this country. It is even more anomalous when one reflects on the passionate arguments and disagreements it has caused.

CONTENDERS FOR CONTROL OVER STANDARDS

The observation that "the whole accrediting movement is a chapter in the struggle for the control of our higher institutions" is as true today as when George F. Zook, then president of the American Council on Education, uttered it twenty years ago.[1] Accrediting is a part of the struggle over standards among contending groups which began with the emergence of universities in the medieval period when the factions were students and teachers, papacy and crown. In this country the contenders have included faculty and trustees, clergy and laity, as well as state and private forces. Of these, no group has been more expressive in its contentions for positions of power than some vociferous faculty members who have continually pleaded for "academic home rule," [2] and likened the modern university with its "struggle between autocratic officers of administration and the democratic personnel of the faculties" [3] to the fascist state.

Cattell, Kirkpatrick, Sinclair, Veblen, and others earlier in this century inveighed against the commercial and financial trustee control of universities. The contemporary clarion call has been broadcast by Louis M. Hacker, a former dean at Columbia University, who contends that:

Professors have been slow to act as citizens within and without the university; and they have permitted its complete governance to fall into the hands of non-academic trustees and regents, legislative authorities and the ever-growing body of university administrators—who both apply and succumb to pressures when times are out of joint.

When universities are directed largely by the professors—backed up by their own constituency—academic freedom in America and academic prestige will have a much better chance of being secure in and outside of "difficult years." [4]

Similarly, university presidents have been vocal in condemning any limitations placed upon their power and authority by the burgeoning accrediting agencies with their formerly uncoordinated and sometimes conflicting, if not unreasonable, demands. Cloyd H. Marvin, for many years president of

[1] Zook (231).   [2] Kirkpatrick (122).   [3] Bourne (22).   [4] Hacker (90).

The George Washington University, expressed the deep conviction of the presidents of most colleges and universities of the country when he said: "Colleges and universities cannot function as trusted, free institutions of higher learning unless their faculties and the administrations representing them are kept from interference by standardizing organizations." [5]

"SEVEN DEVILS"

Undoubtedly the most fearsome talk ever given to a group of representatives of accrediting agencies was the one delivered by Samuel P. Capen in 1939, entitled "Seven Devils in Exchange for One." At the time he had been Specialist for Higher Education in the United States Office of Education, Capen supported the accrediting movement but later, as Chancellor of the University of Buffalo, he consistently and vigorously expressed an opposite point of view.

There are rumblings of revolt, because at long last the worm is turning. Which, being interpreted, means that the responsible administrators of influential institutions in various parts of the country are tired of having the educational and financial policies of their institutions dictated by a horde of irresponsible outsiders, each representing a separate selfish interest.

The issue is plain. Is the American university system to be dominated by competitive blackmail, or is it to be conducted in accordance with the best judgment of the boards and administrative officers charged with this responsibility through charters and through legislative enactments? The American universities gave the standardizing agencies license to live. Whenever the leaders of the universities are ready to unite in the decision that these agencies shall live no longer, they will disappear. I think that day approaches. [6]

Echoes and re-echoes of Capen's famous "seven devils" have reverberated time and time again as numerous presidents, deans, and professors have repeated the admonition that ac-

[5] Marvin (130).   [6] Capen (42).

crediting agencies will have no choice but to fold their tents
and steal away once the leaders in education decide that this
should be done. But that day never arrives. Accreditation is
entwined too tightly in the fabric of higher education to be
unwoven by mere eulogies for the ideal era of the past when
colleges and universities supposedly were untrammeled by
any external controls.

In the midst of contagious fulminations against some of the
restrictions imposed by accrediting agencies, critics have easily
forgotten that controls, both direct and indirect and sometimes deleterious, have been and are being exerted on the
standards of colleges and universities in this country by such
diverse groups as clergy and politicians, industrialists and
labor leaders, sports enthusiasts and foundation officials, as
well as by the philanthropists and alumni whose cultivation
is now a major enterprise in the current search for financial
solvency in higher education. Since these forces of external
control offer inducements more positive than accrediting has
generally provided for an institution already accredited, they
have not been subject to public presidential obloquy.

INDUCEMENTS FOR INSTITUTIONAL ACCREDITATION

On the other hand, the removal or non-attainment of accreditation, whether by a regional association or by one of the
various national professional accrediting agencies, may be a
serious detriment to the welfare of an institution. More than
mere pride and publicity is involved.

Accreditation is included among the requirements for an
institution to become a member of the Association of American
Colleges or the American Council on Education. It is among
the requirements for institutions whose alumnae may be
eligible for membership in the American Association of University Women. With rare exceptions, only accredited institutions are on the approved list from which nominations

may be made for membership in the American Association of University Professors. Accreditation exerts a positive influence on the status of a federal employee under the United States Civil Service regulations, where status depends on whether the individual is a graduate of an accredited or non-accredited institution. In a similar way, the accreditation of programs of study in such fields as architecture, dentistry, engineering, law, medicine, optometry, pharmacy, and veterinary medicine plays an important part in the process of obtaining the required state license to practice one of these professions. Of even more immediate importance to an institution is the fact that grants from foundations and other prospective donors may be withheld from the non-accredited college.

CONFUSION OVER ACCREDITING

Even though accreditation in the United States began well over a half century ago, even though each of the six regional associations of colleges and universities has now assumed accrediting activities, and even though there are approximately thirty national organizations which accredit specific professional fields of study,[7] the concept and implications of accrediting seem to be fully understood by few faculty members and few administrative officers, let alone the general public. Despite the number of accrediting agencies, only a small proportion of individuals from any one faculty are directly involved in any accrediting activities and thus given an opportunity to learn firsthand of its policies and procedures. And the rapid change in top college and university administrative personnel adds to the lack of continuity and of understanding about accrediting on the part of the administrators.[8] For all of these reasons, there have been many misconceptions

[7] See Note 1, p. 96. [8] See Note 2, p. 96.

and much misunderstanding about accrediting, a phenomenon singular to education in the United States.[9]

What actually is accrediting? Basically, *accrediting is the process whereby an organization or agency recognizes a college or university or a program of study as having met certain pre-determined qualifications or standards.*[10]

Despite this simple definition, one individual has accurately described the confusion about accrediting when he speaks of it as

an elusive, nebulous, jellyfish term that means different things to different people and different things to the same people. In trying to bring representatives of various points of view together, it has been most difficult to mediate differences among people who do not agree on what it is on what they do not agree, and, I might add, on which they disagree violently, emotionally and dogmatically. No one, it seems, can be dispassionate about accrediting.[11]

OBSERVATIONS

Accrediting is, basically, a struggle over standards in higher education; individual and group positions are questioned; personal opinions and judgments are involved—all these and other factors have encouraged emotionalism, dogmatism, criticism, and denunciation. Condemnation, however, will neither remove it from the scene nor revise its policies and procedures.

What is needed first is wider comprehension and understanding of the purposes of accrediting and of the part it has played and is playing in the development of our colleges and universities. Only then, on a broad front and in a cooperative manner, can real and needed improvements be made in this native form of control of standards in higher education. To accomplish this will require support, encouragement, and leadership on the part of scholars, administrators, and trustees, as well as the accrediting agencies themselves.

[9] See Note 3, p. 97.   [10] See Note 4, p. 97.   [11] Pinkham (171).

TWO

Control of Standards
in Medieval Times and
in Foreign Countries

JUST AS all Christendom is indebted to
the Middle Ages for the inspiration which led to the building
of cathedrals as monuments to Christianity, so the entire world
owes a debt of gratitude to the medieval genius for the concept
of universities dedicated to the spirit of learning. "The university is a distinctly medieval institution." [1] In its early years
it may have "had no libraries, laboratories or museums, no
endowment or buildings of its own," yet the universities of
the twentieth century are the lineal descendants of the original
twelfth and thirteenth century universities of Bologna or
Paris, Oxford or Cambridge.[2]

[1] Rashdall (178), Vol. 3, p. 458. [2] Haskins (97), p. 2.

7

Our heritage from the medieval universities is not that of buildings or architecture, as in the case of the cathedrals; nor is it the cap and gown, now quite different from the prototype of those earlier days of pomp and ceremony. Rather it is the spirit of inquiry, the association of masters and scholars, the organization of faculties, the creation of a curriculum and examinations leading to a degree, which comprise the university that we have inherited. Our heritage also encompasses the problem of control over standards.

CHURCH CONTROLS

The centers of study, which attracted teachers of reputation as well as students, developed scholarly groups of varied interests which gradually became societies dominated by the masters, as at Paris, or by the students, as at Bologna. At a time when there was no extensive political control by the state over the various classes and groups of people, necessity made it customary for various social groups or guilds to organize and obtain corporate autonomy for their own collective protection and advancement. In this way guilds of masters and of students arose. The societies of masters in time became sufficiently powerful to control admission to their ranks. These guilds of teachers in turn obtained with papal sanction the right of granting or withholding the *licentia docendi*, the license to teach, the degree "with all the rights and privileges pertaining thereto." In other words, the medieval universities, or *studia generalia* as they were known until the fifteenth century, both prepared the students and certified their standard of accomplishment.

At first these centers of study existed without external authority, but in time princes and popes granted charters, officially creating *studia generalia* and extending to masters and students special privileges including exemption from taxation, from military service, and from trial in courts of civil magistrates; in time, many other privileges were granted. Since most students were not native to the location of a particular university and therefore would not have sufficient protection in a local civil court, the exemption from jurisdiction of the civil courts was particularly important as an inducement to attract students. For an institution to obtain important and adequate recognition outside of its own domain, a grant by papal bull or royal order was required—as the *ius ubique docendi*, the right to teach anywhere, was dependent on such a grant, and was essential to the tutor who wished to be accepted in a guild of masters.

Not only was it important for the universities to have papal or royal support, but it also was important for both church and lay authorities to seek the allegiance of the universities, since these two groups sparred with each other for political supremacy. Consequently, popes vied with kings in granting privileges to the universities, which thus were able to maintain a degree of relative autonomy throughout the struggle for their control, which continued for several centuries. And, it should be remembered, this was at a time when scholars were taking a leading part in shaping the ideas of the Church and when the Church held undisputed domination over western thought and culture.

NEW EDUCATIONAL AUTHORITY

The domination of the Church, however, did not remain constant. Men's ideas were enlarged as trade increased with the East and eventually with all parts of the world, as the invention of the printing press increased literacy, and as the growing power of city states and nations changed and eventually replaced the feudal structure of society and challenged the political influence of the Church. By the sixteenth century the Reformation threatened not only the political power but the spiritual authority of the Church as well. In so doing it both destroyed the unity of European society and thought which had existed for a millennium and created the need for a new educational authority.

During the fifteenth century the universities had declined in influence and position because of their overemphasis on clericalism, obsolete methods, undue deference to authority and a dearth of able scholars. Certain external conditions, such as growing nationalism, the great schism in the Catholic hierarchy, and widespread wars and political confusion also diminished their status. Consequently, by the sixteenth century the older universities seemed incapable of facing the intellectual ferment taking place in Western culture, while the newer universities of Geneva, Scotland, and the Netherlands made almost a clean break with the traditions of the Middle Ages. In Protestant lands the universities were easily dominated by civil authority, and toward the end of this century "the doctrine of the supremacy of the state and the complete dependence of all other groups on state sanction became the accepted legal theory." [3] Thus the basis was laid for the university to serve the state as an instrument of national interest.

For the next two centuries the universities served the state more like sleeping beauties, becoming havens for theological debate, rather than centers of inquiry and learning. In an era of enlightenment influenced by such men as Descartes and Hobbes, Newton and Leibnitz, Locke, Voltaire, and Diderot as well as Montesquieu, Rousseau, and Adam Smith, the learned world was identified with society, not with educational institutions. The universities went their peaceful way, catering to the young men of birth and breeding, concentrating attention not on the discovery of new learning but merely on the preservation of the old. Even though the universities of France and England were less affected by the European move-

[3] Brody (28), p. 7.

ment towards *étatism,* they too were intellectually uninspir-
ing places. At Oxford in the eighteenth century, "the ancient
faculties had disappeared; law and medicine had migrated to
London; theology slumbered. Oxford and Cambridge [were]
shut off from the professional stream for a hundred and fifty
years." [4]

Fortunately, yet in some ways unfortunately, the indolent
atmosphere of many of the universities was altered by their
regeneration in the nineteenth century. The renewed life
began in Germany after the Napoleonic victory in 1806 at
Jena. Largely under the stimulation of such men as Fichte,
Prussia aroused itself from defeat by concentrating its efforts
on building the state and subordinating all activities, including
that of the universities, to this new spirit of nationalism. The
University of Berlin, founded in 1810 under state supervision
and financial support, epitomized the new emphasis on scholarship, research, and pure knowledge and influenced not only
the universities of Germany but the future direction of university education throughout the world. During this century,
through the leadership of von Humboldt and others, the
German universities became famous as centers of philosophical
speculation and scientific research; they attracted students and
scholars from far and wide, many of whom returned to their
native lands with a well nourished desire to transmit to their
fellow countrymen the spirit of unfettered inquiry and learning. But Germany's academic leadership could not be maintained. It finally succumbed in the twentieth century to the
overwhelming influence of pan-Germanism and the insidious
power of degenerate nationalism.

MINISTRIES OF EDUCATION

In France the swath of destruction of the Revolution carried
away in 1793 the educational system and with it the univer-

4 Conant (51).

sities of the *ancien régime*. In 1808 the university did reappear, but in a new form and under state control, when Napoleon with his emphasis on centralization and orderliness created the Université de France and a permanent system of public instruction under the supervision of a Ministry of Education. This control by the state of education and educational standards has continued with only slight modifications through each of the many governments of nineteenth and twentieth century France. The state remains as the dominating force by providing almost three-fourths of the income of the universities, by controlling the number of professorships and making appointments, by deciding the promotions in rank and the salary scale, and by requiring that candidates for officially recognized degrees and for admission to the professions pass state examinations. Consequently, in France as in other European countries, the "universities are less responsive to public opinion and less directly affected by general social developments than are the universities of the United States, public or private. Traditionally, French institutions have remained largely aloof from the contemporary social scene," as their doors have been open to a limited number, the intellectual élite chosen through a highly competitive and selective process." [5]

This form of control for institutions of higher learning—whereby ministries of education are assigned broad powers of policy and administration, and the admission and right to practice a profession is restricted to those who pass state examinations—is found with varying modifications in the countries of continental Europe, in the Arab countries of the Near East, and in fact in almost all countries throughout the world except those where British influence has been predominant. Such a form of control provides both an effective means of rapidly altering academic standards and an administrative

[5] Newburn (148).

organization that can be described relatively easily. It also provides a common basis in reaching agreements for international recognition of degrees and professional qualifications, such as is contemplated among the six nations in the European Economic Community. On the other hand, this method of administration can readily be adapted to the desires of a state which wishes to convert the universities into instruments of extreme nationalism. We have seen this path followed in Fascist Italy and Nazi Germany. We are now seeing it pursued in Russia and other Communist countries where the ministries of education possess broad, centralized authority and where the Communist Party exerts dictatorial influence over the content of lectures and subjects taught. This subservience of education to the nation was described by Adlai E. Stevenson following an extensive trip to Russia: "Service to the state . . . is the objective of the entire intellectual and educational apparatus of the Soviet Union." [6]

EXTERNAL EXAMINATIONS

In contrast, emphasis on academic freedom and the development of the individual has been stronger in Great Britain than in any other country. Favored by a tradition and history of autonomy, the British universities have in the main been controlled by the faculties who, however, have had to be nudged from time to time by intermittent royal commissions of inquiry into a greater awareness of contemporary social needs. Sharing with some continental universities a long era of intellectual torpor, Oxford and Cambridge, which had been under ecclesiastical domination, were revived during the nineteenth century as a result of internal stirrings and of acts of Parliament, including the Test Act of 1871 which removed as a requirement for taking degrees and for faculty appointment membership in the Church of England.

[6] *New York Times,* November 21, 1958.

In more recent years, under economic necessity, the national government has been forced to take drastic steps to support higher education for which it now furnishes close to 70 per cent of the revenues, in addition to funds for scholarships. The University Grants Committee, an autonomous body created in 1919 to allocate government funds among the universities and not required to report to the Treasury, has the power of deciding the size of the various institutions, their rate of expansion, and even their curricular additions. Despite the immense proportion of educational revenue emanating from the government and despite "the conversion of Britain's vigorously individualistic system of higher education into an instrument of national policy," it is still possible to claim that the universities "remain independent and have experienced no interference with their operation." [7]

The nations in the British Commonwealth, in addition to a tradition and history of respect for academic autonomy, have inherited from the English a feature of university control which is distinct not only from the practice pursued on the European continent but from that of the United States. Following the custom developed in the Middle Ages, an institution wishing to award degrees must be granted a charter for this purpose by the appropriate legal authority. Not only have such charters been severely limited in England—Oxford and Cambridge were the only degree-granting institutions until 1836—but customarily before an institution is assigned degree-granting authority (that is, the power to establish academic standards), it is required to serve first as a university college, an affiliate of a legally chartered university. In this relationship, as was the case with the present University of Durham when it was organized in 1832 as an affiliate of Oxford, the new institution has only the responsibility of teaching, not that of examining. The latter responsibility rests with the university

[7] Newman (153).

until such time as the affiliated institution is considered to be sufficiently mature academically to warrant a charter as a university with the accompanying powers of examining and granting degrees.

This method of maintaining standards, developed by the British and followed by the Commonwealth nations as their answer to the question of control, has been well served by the University of London. Chartered in 1836 as an external examining authority for what are now the British civic universities, the University of London subsequently enrolled students of its own and continued its original purpose of examining students and awarding degrees not only on a national but on a worldwide basis. This method of control provided a means of maintaining university standards in an empire on which the sun never set.

In such countries as Australia, Canada, India, New Zealand, and Pakistan, the practice of affiliation is followed today. In India, with over nine hundred institutions of higher learning, there are only some thirty degree-granting universities—including, for example, the University of Bombay which a few years ago alone had ninety-one affiliated institutions. In Canada, where strong British and French traditions "have been modified by North American social and environmental conditions" [8] to create a somewhat varied pattern of control, there are only fifty-one active degree granting universities and colleges out of almost three hundred institutions offering courses of university standards.[9] It is through these few pre-eminent institutions—Oxford and Cambridge, the University of London and other more recent universities—that control of standards in higher education in these countries has been maintained.

[8] Canadian Universities (37).   [9] See Note 5, p. 97.

OBSERVATIONS

In comparison to the orderliness and relative simplicity of both the Continental and British systems of establishing and maintaining university standards, the method developed in the United States appears confusing and filled with conflicts. Accrediting, the result of a singular pattern of social forces in this country, is based upon the principle of a balance of political powers with decentralized authority. This is in marked contrast to the social forces and political principles of other countries which led them to rely either on ministries of education or the use of external examinations for the control of academic standards. Only through a knowledge of the Continental and British systems and their heritage can one fully appreciate the function of accrediting in the United States.

THREE

Native Heritage and Traditions

Both on the continent of Europe and in England the history of higher education has involved the redirection of the universities, many of which were founded in the Middle Ages. In contrast, the record in America has been quite different. Here—with only an indirect heritage from the medieval university but with an immediate dependence upon the Protestant university traditions of England and Scotland—the imprint of geography and economics, religion and politics was indelibly inscribed on our colleges and on our later universities as they were freshly created in a manner distinct from, even though related to, their earlier prototypes. In no feature is this more apparent than in the area of control of academic standards.

Accreditation, the contemporary form of control of academic standards which has been developed in the United

States, is totally distinct from that provided by ministries of education or by systems of external examinations. To understand how this singular phenomenon germinated in the late nineteenth century and then pollinated in the twentieth, it is necessary first to consider some of the social forces that helped to shape higher education in this country as its orientation developed from a small, precarious, denominationally directed, frontier college to the present day university, world renowned for its catholicity of viewpoint and breadth of scholarship.

COLONIAL INFLUENCES

In Colonial America, peopled almost entirely by dissenting Protestants, attention to collegiate education was prompted as much by the social and intellectual background of colonial leaders as it was by the need for an educated ministry. Possessing no endowments and inheriting no guild of scholars, the colleges in this country through necessity were organized by boards of trustees, composed mostly of clergymen and philanthropic laymen. In their early days, both Harvard College and the College of William and Mary attempted to establish a basis of internal control, as at Oxford and Cambridge, in which the faculties would have paramount influence; but these attempts failed. The relatively weak position of the college tutors, the proprietary instinct of the founders, and particularly the clerical insistence upon orthodoxy combined to establish trustee control as the accepted pattern, with a president serving in a position between trustees and faculty.

Although some Colonial colleges obtained official recognition from the Crown to legalize their status, Harvard, with the support of the Massachusetts General Court and in the Scottish tradition, influenced the course of higher education in this country by operating and granting degrees without a royal charter. Consequently, instead of being the controlling factor over the existence or non-existence of a college, charters in many later cases merely acted to confirm the existence of a college that already had been performing those functions, including the granting of degrees, which in Europe and England could have been discharged only by a chartered university. With no practical legal restriction, it was possible for colleges to be created by lay boards of trustees spurred by the influence of religious sectarianism, geographic separation, and local pride, without regard to actual educational needs. In contrast to England, where for centuries there were only two degree-granting institutions, in Colonial America there ultimately were nine colleges awarding academic degrees. By the 1830's, when the third English university was chartered, the United States boasted of more than fifty colleges granting degrees, providing education in a wide geographical area and yet competing with one another for students in a manner unknown in any other country.

During the century and a half between the founding of Harvard and the adoption of the Federal Constitution, twenty-four colleges were created of which five were what we would today call public.[1] However, the distinctions between the public and the private colleges were few, relatively unimportant, and of little concern to the people at the time. At all institutions the presidents were customarily ministers, as were most of the faculty and trustees, the curriculums varied little, and financial support came from both public and private sources. In fact, the institutions that we now know as Columbia University and the University of Pennsylvania were each for a time actually under public control.[2] These and other colleges, such as Bowdoin, Hamilton, Harvard, Hobart, Union, and Yale, received large sums of money from the public treasuries.[3] Williams College, as an example, owed

[1] Millett (137), p. 91.   [2] Council of State Governments (57), p. 15.
[3] Blackmar (18).

its continued existence to the Commonwealth of Massachusetts which over the years, until the 1890's, was the institution's largest single benefactor even though the last actual grant from the state was made in 1863.[4] With no defined separation between public and private colleges and with wide acceptance of the principle of church and local support for education, the Constitution of the United States included no reference to education.

NO CONSTITUTIONAL PROVISION

In fact, at the time of the Constitutional Convention "education had not as yet arisen to be a sufficiently important matter of public policy"[5] to warrant specific mention in the final document, which John Quincy Adams called "a bundle of compromises."[6] Even though the American Philosophical Society supported a national system of education, and such various individuals as Samuel Knox, Benjamin Rush, Samuel H. Smith, and Noah Webster wrote publicly in favor of it, the tradition of religion and sectarianism and the influence of geographical separation and decentralization were too strong to support such a radical departure from "the then prevailing view of education as a private, or a religious, or a philanthropic function."[7] With the adoption in 1791 of the Tenth Amendment, education—as one of the powers "not delegated to the United States" and not prohibited to the states by the Constitution—was considered to be a state and local responsibility. Therefore, it was the state governments to whom the colleges and universities turned for their charters, and it is these charters which have provided the institutions with considerable protection from political interference and government dictation.

[4] Rudolph (191), p. 193.   [5] Reisner (188).   [6] Farrand (79), p. 201.
[7] Spurlock (204), p. 15.

The inviolability of a state charter was tested and supported in the famous Dartmouth College case of 1819 which Charles A. Beard has described as

a spectacular event more important in American educational history than the founding of any single institution of higher learning.

By securing the boards of trustees of endowed educational institutions against political interference, the Dartmouth decision in effect decreed that a large part of the terrain of the higher learning should be forever occupied and controlled by private corporations composed of citizens empowered to select their own successors, collect and disburse money, choose presidents and professors, and more or less directly determine the letter and spirit of the curriculum.[8]

Although there is some difference of opinion as to the extent of influence the Dartmouth decision had on subsequent developments in higher education, there is no question that it laid the basis for the distinction between public and private colleges and indirectly but ultimately led to the Morrill Act of 1862. Also, there is no question that it supported the independence of innumerable sectarian colleges as they sprouted like mushrooms in the footsteps of the early settlers migrating westward across the Appalachian Mountains to the immense Mississippi Valley and the Great Plains beyond.

The survival of these colleges, however, proved to be quite another matter. Financial disaster, denominational competition, unfavorable location, internal dissension, fires, and storms took their toll. Of the colleges founded before the Civil War in sixteen states, over four-fifths either died sudden deaths or withered away.[9] Despite this high mortality, 268 institutions—the vast majority of them private—did survive from the post-Constitution pre-Civil War era, in addition to the twenty-four

---

[8] Beard (16), Vol. 1, p. 819; also, see Note 6, p. 97. [9] Tewksbury (208), p. 27.

institutions founded prior to the Constitution.[10] Eternal optimism, religious fervor, and local pride stimulated this continual founding of institutions of so-called higher education; and the generative process was nourished by sectarian diversity, an anti-mercantilistic philosophy of laissez-faire, unique military security, a federal political system of non-intervention by government, and an extensive geography with regional differences and slow communication. The seed-beds of diversity in higher education were well planted, but before this diversity could blossom, as it did by the end of the nineteenth century, major revisions in the curriculum had to be made.

COMMON CURRICULUMS

Not only were the seventeenth and eighteenth century Colonial colleges partially dependent for support upon British philanthropy, but they adopted a curriculum which differed little from that pursued at Oxford and Cambridge at a time when the English universities were already "waxing feeble." [11] This curriculum, with its heavy overtones of clerical control, was comprised of Greek and Latin, mathematics and logic, and moral and natural philosophy, and it persisted with minor variations until the Civil War. No colleges were more committed to this program of study than Yale and Princeton, and no colleges exerted more influence in the founding of other colleges than did these two academically and religiously conservative institutions. Their conservative position was given ample expression in the Yale Report of 1828 which has been called "the most influential publication in the whole history of American higher education between the Revolution and the Civil War." [12]

Authorized by the president and the fellows of Yale, who were concerned with the need for revising the requirements

---

[10] Millett (137), p. 91. [11] Bryce (33), Vol. II, p. 711. [12] Brubacher and Rudy (31), p. 101.

of the "dead languages," members of the faculty reported among other things that "a prescribed curriculum, featuring 'the thorough study of the ancient languages,' was the only proper system for a college." [13] This report not only reinforced the blanket of conservatism which was impeding the growth of academic diversity but served also as historic proof of the statement that "changing the curriculum entails all the physical and psychological difficulties of moving a cemetery." [14]

It follows that a college which originally catered to a particular segment of society and was "not organically knit into the fabric of economic life" would be slow to respond to social changes.[15] Such was the situation with the majority of pre-Civil War colleges, especially the more influential ones along the Eastern seaboard, until declining enrollments forced more attention to social needs.

Francis Wayland, president of Brown University, having noted that "the proportion of college graduates to the whole population" was decreasing and having felt the impact of this trend on the budget of his own institution, in 1850 recommended drastic changes in the curriculum which the Corporation soon adopted.[16] An earlier report in 1841 embodied the basis of these recommendations in the following statement:

An effort must soon be made by the more advanced colleges to adapt their courses to the different capacities and wants of students, giving to each officer the opportunity to carry his course of instruction to as great a degree of perfection as he is able, fixing certain acquisitions as necessary to graduation but making such arrangements as will enable those not candidates for a degree to obtain in the various departments of knowledge such instruction as may qualify them for the occupations for which they are designed.[17]

These changes at Brown, the introduction in the 1850's of

---

[13] *Ibid.*, also, Storr (205), pp. 29-31. [14] Abbott (1), p. 5. [15] Hofstadter and Hardy (105), p. 21. [16] Bronson (29), p. 262. [17] *Ibid.*, p. 267.

parallel courses to provide flexibility in the curriculum at Harvard, Yale, Dartmouth, Rochester, and Michigan, modifications in the admission requirements, and the founding of a few technological institutions, were various measures taken to try and meet the social demands for more education for greater numbers of students in an expanding democracy. But these measures were insufficient.

GOVERNMENT ACTION

As a result of the Dartmouth College decision, chartered colleges could not be altered by government action, and in accordance with amendments to many state constitutions, public funds after the 1840's could not generally be granted to religious institutions, which included most of the colleges then in existence.[18] However, the Federal Congress, whose interest was aroused, could make provisions for the establishment of colleges to meet the needs of "the people" and this it did with popular support through the passage of the land-grant college act of 1862. Thus the Pandora's box of diversity in education, with all its blessings and all its ills, was pried open by government action.

This legislation, one of the major influences in the transformation of higher learning in the United States, was not, however, the initial expression of government interest in education. Not only did the Ordinance of 1785 and the more famous Northwest Ordinance of 1787 make specific reference to education but subsequent to 1800, provision was made for land to be granted to help support state universities in all but a few states as they were admitted to the Union.[19] Despite vigorous opposition from private and denominational institutions, state universities—such as the influential universities of Virginia and Michigan—which in their early days were hardly distinguishable from private colleges, increased to twenty by

[18] Cowley (64), p. 75. [19] Thwing (209), p. 180.

the time of the Civil War. They and the land-grant colleges with their emphasis on agricultural and mechanic arts represented the growing philosophy of higher education for everyone who qualified and not merely for the well-born and the professionally inclined. These were the institutions which made the first impressive breach in the classical curriculum by their development of programs of study for the future farmer, engineer, merchant, and manager. But other forces as well undermined the heritage of a standard curriculum for all college students.

EXPANSION OF KNOWLEDGE

The industrial revolution of the nineteenth century was accompanied by the growing importance of science and technology and an enormous expansion of systematized knowledge which under one pretext or another was woven into the teaching by some of the more alert college professors. And the expansion of knowledge was stimulated no more profoundly than by Charles Darwin. It has been said that "the impact of Darwin on religion was shattering" and "his impact on philosophy was revolutionary." [20] It could also be said that his impact on the classical curriculum of the liberal arts college was explosive.

Finding it difficult both to reconcile their religious beliefs with scientific discoveries and to provide adequate funds to support the colleges in an era of profound social change, the clerics lost their former dominant influence and gave way to men of academic specialization on the faculties and to men of business and finance on the boards of trustees. These new trustees, indebted to the industrial revolution for their fortunes, were generally more sensitive to the need for science and technology in the college curriculum. They furnished the financial support needed to increase the college faculties

[20] Commager (49), p. 83.

and enlarge the course offerings without which Charles W. Eliot could never have successfully introduced the Harvard elective system. This free elective system, which has been called "a beautiful instrument for a reformer," [21] influenced curriculums on college campuses throughout the land. In turn, it supplied the means of breaking the academic lock step and of gradually enlarging the secondary school courses of study to care for the rapidly increasing school population with its varied educational and vocational interests.[22] By the turn of the century the elective principle had begun to destroy the main standardizing influence in higher education—the classical liberal arts curriculum—that had existed in this country for almost two and a half centuries.

PHILOSOPHY OF LAISSEZ-FAIRE

The influence of the laissez-faire philosophy, so prominent during the nineteenth century in industry and finance, can thus be discerned in the development of the elective system, as it also can be perceived in the creation between 1860 and 1890 of over two hundred institutions freely chartered with few restrictions by any state as to courses to be offered or degrees granted.[23] Colleges founded for all sorts of reasons competed with each other for students, and in the competition not infrequently extended themselves beyond their academic and financial capabilities. Many of these institutions, not merely to offer proper preparation for college but to increase their enrollment and income as well, enrolled preparatory students, and by so doing frequently lowered the standards of their courses and remained out of touch with the secondary schools.[24] This situation led a representative of the French Ministry of Education to say at the Columbian Exposition in

[21] Pierson (167), p. 85. [22] See Note 7, p. 98. [23] Millett (137), p. 91. [24] See Note 8, p. 98.

1893 that in the United States "the distinction between second-ary and higher education is not clearly established." [25]

While many colleges were partially preparatory schools, others were striving valiantly to become universities in fact as well as in name. Early in the nineteenth century George Ticknor and others made the initial efforts to introduce German scholarship and graduate studies into the pattern of American higher education. But it required a change in social conditions, an increase in wealth, the development of science and the scientific method, and the experience of hundreds, if not thousands, of scholars returning after their training in Germany to build the foundations of the universities which began to appear only by the 1870's and 1880's.

With the exception of a few institutions such as Clark and Johns Hopkins, which were created specifically to offer graduate work, the foundations of the future universities were merely superimposed on already existing colleges whose edu-cational structures had been fashioned in most cases to offer a simple, common, classical curriculum. The combination of these two elements, traditional undergraduate education and German scholarly graduate studies, helped further to en-courage such extremes in diversity that few academic standards were widely acknowledged.

Along with graduate education, professional education de-veloped but under a more severe handicap. Training for the ancient and influential professions of law and medicine had for many years in the United States been conducted first by the apprentice system and then by proprietary schools whose owners and lecturers had no connections with universities and who for the sake of their own financial advantage wished to have none. As strenuous efforts were made to improve professional education and associate it with the universities, and as the professions rapidly multiplied, another dimension

[25] Harris (96), 1895-96, Vol. 2, p. 1154.

was added to the already growing diversity of higher education in the United States. In all directions the need became evident for some force which would develop and enforce academic standards.

OBSERVATIONS

The panorama of collegiate education at the turn of the past century presents a scene of active confusion: students being enrolled in increasing numbers from more secondary schools by institutions being founded at a rapid rate—normal schools, teachers colleges, junior colleges, technological institutes, schools of art, conservatories of music, professional schools, liberal arts colleges, universities—offering courses from agriculture to zoology. All this, but with no commonly accepted academic standards or admission requirements, and even no common definition of a college. It is no wonder that in a speech entitled "Academic Standards versus Individual Differences—the Dilemma of Democratic Education," C. M. McConn, then dean at Lehigh University, has said:

American education at the end of the last century had come to be a variegated hodgepodge of uncoordinated practices—in school and college alike—which had never undergone any screening from anybody, and many which were shoddy, futile, and absurd beyond anything we now conceive of; and the Age of Standards—as the period from 1890 to 1915 may come to be called—brought order out of chaos.[26]

How this chaos, confusion, and ferment was resolved, at least partially, is the story of accrediting.

[26] McConn (131).

FOUR

Institutional Reformation

IT HAS been said of American educational institutions that they "respond more to social needs and pressures than to first principles." [1] In no phase of higher education does this comment seem to be more relevant than in accreditation. Created in part by the colleges and universities themselves to counteract certain excesses that were rapidly developing in the United States at the end of the nineteenth century, accrediting in its manifold attempts at reformation eventually exceeded the bounds of reasonableness and in turn needed to be constrained for its excesses and attempts at over-standardization.

Opinion differs as to which organization first employed accrediting as a means of external control of educational standards. The University of Michigan,[2] the Association of

---

[1] Hook (108). [2] Monroe (140), p. 1.

American Medical Colleges,[3] the American Association of University Women,[4] and the University Senate of the Methodist Episcopal Church [5] each has its supporters for this mark of distinction. However, the Board of Regents of the University of the State of New York, which has been called "the most influential standardizing organ in existence" [6] holds unquestioned title to this historic recognition. By legislation enacted in 1787, members of the New York State Board of Regents were required "to visit every College in this State once a year" and report yearly to the Legislature.[7] In this way the foundations for accrediting were laid a hundred years before it was developed as an answer to the burgeoning diversity of education and the lack of coordination among the multiplying number of high schools and colleges.

REGIONAL ASSOCIATIONS

Although conditions in education in the 1870's, 1880's and 1890's were basically the same throughout the country, there were sufficient regional variations that different approaches were developed to meet the two general problems of standards and college admissions. Faced with the necessity of preparing their students for separate college examinations, no two of which were necessarily based on the same syllabus, members of the Massachusetts Classical and High School Teachers Association in 1884 initiated a conference with Charles W. Eliot at Harvard. This led to the creation in 1885 of the New England Association of Colleges and Secondary Schools, the first "attempt in this country to bring together for the common good educators and educational institutions from the same geographical area." [8] The success of this endeavor prompted the Michigan Schoolmasters' Club in 1894 to ap-

[3] Kelly (119).   [4] Talbot and Rosenberry (207), p. 94.   [5] Limbert (126), p. 112.   [6] Capen (40), p. 114.   [7] Abbott (2), p. 23; also, Horner (109), p. 1. [8] New England Association (149), p. 3.

proach James B. Angell, president of the University of Michigan, with the idea of forming a similar organization in that area of the country. The following year at a meeting held at Northwestern University, the North Central Association of Colleges and Secondary Schools was organized for the purpose of establishing "closer relations between the colleges and the secondary schools"; at the first annual meeting discussion was centered on the problems of college admissions and the distinction between a college and a secondary school.[9]

In 1870-1871 the University of Michigan, as the only state university without a preparatory department of the twenty-three then in existence, had adopted the German practice of sending at regular intervals certain members of its faculty to inspect the high schools and pass judgment or certify them as to their ability to prepare students for the university. This method of secondary school accreditation, which at the time had the support of both the schoolmasters and the university faculty, was adopted within a decade in a half dozen other middle western states although under varying administrative aegis.[10] This procedure helped to improve standards, helped to make a state system of education a reality, and provided another basis for the later widespread practice of collegiate accreditation.

In contrast to the New England and North Central associations where the initiative for organization came from the secondary school people, the impetus in the Middle Atlantic states and the South was found among the college men who themselves recognized the need to establish closer relations and to elevate standards. The College Association of Pennsylvania, having been created in 1887 to encourage passage by the state legislature of an act "to render impossible further taxation of property used for educational purposes," soon

[9] North Central Association (155), 1895.   [10] See Note 9, p. 98.

realized that the association could profitably be extended to include institutions from a wider geographical area.[11] Thus the Middle States Association of Colleges and Secondary Schools, as it is known today, became a reality in 1889 although secondary school members were not added until four years later.

In the South, at the same time as the North Central Association was being organized, a small group of college leaders formed what is now called the Southern Association of Colleges and Secondary Schools, for which James H. Kirkland, chancellor of Vanderbilt University, served initially and for many years as the guiding light and mentor. The chaotic problems of standards and college admissions in the South were similar to those in the rest of the country in kind, but not in extent. The destruction of the Civil War which still continues to plague the advancement of education in the South presented more serious issues than any other regional association has had to face.[12] Not only did most of the colleges for women accept students with only a few years of preparatory work, but many of them even granted credit toward a degree for these sub-college studies. One of the leading southern state universities for many years was not eligible for membership in the association because of its extremely low entrance requirements. As a result of these and other factors, the Southern Association has continually been forced to look to the North Central and the Middle States associations for guidance in its endeavors to raise academic standards. And it is from these two associations that the leadership in regional accrediting has come.

CERTIFICATION OR ENTRANCE EXAMINATIONS

While the University of Michigan's pattern of certifying high schools was spreading in the Middle West, a different

[11] Middle States Association (136), 1887.   [12] See Note 10, p. 98.

emphasis in the articulation of preparatory schools and colleges was emerging in the East where the state universities were less influential and where preparatory schools distinct from colleges were more prevalent. Here the emphasis was on the development of standard examinations which the colleges would accept in lieu of their own separately designed and individually administered entrance tests. The New York Board of Regents by 1878 had adopted a system of examinations for secondary school students to serve as a basis both for graduation from high school and for admission to some of the colleges of the state. Following this pattern, Eliot of Harvard and Nicholas Murray Butler of Columbia, first independently and then cooperatively, made proposals which led after some years to the Middle States Association in 1899 officially recommending what came to be called the College Entrance Examination Board. At the 1901 meeting of the Middle States Association, Butler was able to report that the College Board had been in existence for a year, and that as a result of the cooperation among the secondary schools and colleges in creating this new agency, there was more assurance of stability of definition in college admission subjects.

In New England some colleges, partially for fear of not attracting sufficient numbers of students, did not accept the College Board examinations as the basis for admission. In 1902 these other colleges formed the New England College Entrance Certificate Board, distinct from the New England Association of Colleges and Secondary Schools. Largely because of a lack of finances this new organization did not inspect schools; rather, it granted the privilege of recommending a student for college admission to the principals of those schools whose previous graduates had done well in the first half of their freshman year in college.

Other groups and organizations also were concerned with standards and college admission requirements. The National

Education Association, which according to Butler was then "a great force in the intellectual life of the profession," appointed a series of committees, the first of which, the Committee of Ten under the chairmanship of Eliot, in 1893 "marked the beginning of the complete reorganization of the relationships between secondary schools and colleges in this country." [13] Through these committees and other forces, increasing attention was being given to the curriculum of the high school, the majority of whose students were no longer entering college. And as the high school and college course offerings became more diversified the question of admissions and standards grew more complicated.

ATTEMPT AT COOPERATION

By 1905 George E. MacLean, president of the State University of Iowa, convinced that coordinated attention to these issues was warranted, proposed to the National Association of State Universities that a meeting of representatives of certain educational associations be convened to try to find solutions for some of the problems. From this proposal developed the National Conference Committee on Standards of Colleges and Secondary Schools which met initially in 1906 at Williamstown, Massachusetts with representatives present from the four regional associations, the College Entrance Examination Board, the New England College Entrance Certificate Board, and the National Association of State Universities. Within two years the committee began the custom of holding its annual meeting in the New York offices of the recently created Carnegie Foundation for the Advancement of Teaching with the president of the foundation and the United States Commissioner of Education in attendance.

During its seventeen years of existence the National Conference Committee deliberated over a wide range of topics

[13] Butler (35), pp. 195, 197.

related to admissions and standards. At one time it even considered the proposition of dividing the country into seven areas with an inspector assigned to each area. But its greatest contribution was in providing a means of communication and coordination among the organizations which its members represented and in adopting and recommending definitions which became widely accepted. None of the definitions which it formulated has received more attention than the one which defined a unit as representing "a year's study in any subject in a secondary school, constituting approximately a quarter of a full year's work." [14] Soon adopted by the Carnegie Foundation, this definition has been known ever since, despite protests from the foundation, as the Carnegie unit.

INFLUENCE OF CARNEGIE FOUNDATION

During this period of educational anarchy another force for the establishment of educational standards appeared on the scene. Founded in 1905 by one of the great industrial monarchs, the Carnegie Foundation for the Advancement of Teaching was organized initially for the purpose of providing retirement allowances to college professors. To support such a non-contributory project as was undertaken at that time would today, in a period of steady inflation, present an almost insurmountable problem of obtaining sufficient funds. At that time the major problem was not one of finances. Rather it was the definition of a college. For the foundation to provide retirement allowances to college professors, an adequate definition of a college was a basic necessity.

Henry S. Pritchett, in his first annual report as president of the foundation, stated that "the terms college and university have, as yet, no fixed meaning on this continent." Consequently Pritchett and other members of the board, in their search of a definition for a college, turned to the one employed

14 Nat. Conf. Com. (145), 1909.

by the New York State Board of Regents. In the application of this definition the Carnegie trustees were accused for many years of being a standardizing or accrediting agency, to which Pritchett replied that "the only standards that the Foundation has urged upon institutions of learning have been those of common honesty and sincerity." [15]

But these standards for many institutions were beyond what they then were practicing. It took what now seems to have been an inordinate length of time for the colleges to realize that their standards had to be raised and that in the American political tradition only the colleges themselves could accomplish this. For this purpose the stronger, more reputable institutions resorted to accreditation, the American form of control over academic standards, as the means of assuring better education to the public and of protecting themselves against the pretentious, shoddy, even fraudulent institutions which often called themselves colleges or universities.

The chaotic conditions of this period prompted Woodrow Wilson, then president of Princeton University, to proclaim in 1907:

We are on the eve of a period of reconstruction. We are on the eve of a period when we are going to set up standards. We are on the eve of a period of synthesis, when, tired of this dispersion and standardless analysis, we are going to put things together into something like a connected and thought-out scheme of endeavor. It is inevitable. . . .[16]

INEVITABILITY OF ACCREDITING

From the vantage point of a half century, it was inevitable that the North Central Association would eventually require institutions seeking membership to be inspected and meet stated requirements—in other words, to be accredited. The pattern of certification and inspection of high schools, fol-

[15] Pritchett (175). [16] Wilson (222).

lowed for some time by most of the Middle Western states, provided an excellent foundation for the inauguration of the program in 1905 by that association on a regional basis for secondary schools. With the diversity that was developing and the chaotic standards that existed among colleges and universities, it was logical that accrediting would be extended to higher institutions—as was done when the first list of regionally accredited institutions was issued by the North Central Association in 1913. It was equally logical that the standards adopted would be similar to those then being employed by the influential Carnegie Foundation and the United States Bureau of Education, both of which organizations by necessity could use only standards that were specific, factual, and mechanical.

Once started, accrediting was bound to spread into additional areas of the country where other measures were not proving adequate in creating and maintaining standards of education. Following a number of years of debate and deliberation, resolutions and appointments of committees, the Southern Association incorporated accrediting as a part of its required procedures and completed its first list of accredited colleges and universities in 1919, although not without belated protests. Encountering similar hesitation and uncertainty the Middle States Association issued its first list in 1921 after a prolonged debate at the annual meeting that year as to whether or not the list should be made public.

The colleges and universities of New England, overcoming an attempt in the early 1920's to introduce accrediting, were able to retain "a cherished sense of individuality, accompanied by an unmistakable unwillingness to be subjected to the critical scrutiny of outsiders," until 1952, when after a sharp debate and over the determined opposition of the presidents of a few leading universities, the association voted to begin formal accreditation.[17] In contrast, the Northwest Association of Secondary and Higher Schools, established in 1917 under predominant secondary school influence, quickly responded to the example of the North Central Association by adopting within a period of only several years both its practice and its standards of accrediting. The last regional association to be organized, the Western College Association, began in 1924 on the Pomona College campus as an informal group of Southern California college administrators and not until 1948, after it had expanded its membership into a formal organization, did it vote for accreditation.[18]

CHANGES IN EMPHASIS OF REGIONAL ACCREDITING

During the nearly half century that accrediting has been conducted by one or more of the regional associations, changes in its basic purpose have taken place. No longer is the emphasis on college admission requirements. The early committees of the National Education Association, the subsequent activities of the regional associations and other educational organizations, and the development and wide use of aptitude tests have brought some orderliness out of the once variegated admissions situation. No longer is there the same relative emphasis on the maintenance of standards—particularly specific, detailed standards. Through an almost continuous barrage of criticisms, accrediting has helped to bring about an elevation in the quality of education and a broad acceptance of the general concept of what constitutes a good college or university. Because of this accomplishment various organizations, such as the American Association of Junior Colleges, the National Catholic Educational Association and the several Protestant church boards of education, which at one time or another had active interests in accrediting, have largely placed their reliance for such matters on the regional associations. Even the in-

[17] New England Association (149), p. 7. [18] See Note 11, p. 98.

dependent American Association of University Women was willing in recent years to make substantial modifications in its practices of three quarters of a century and to grant more recognition to the standards of regional accrediting. But these accomplishments have not been attained without contentions and disputes.

From their inception the regional associations have been beset with the issue of their own control and the issue of the standards which they enforce. The chasmal schism between liberal education and teacher education which has plagued higher education in the United States all too long showed itself even at the initial meeting of the Middle States Association in 1887, and it was not until 1934 that this association would accredit teachers colleges. In the North Central Association, standards for teachers colleges were adopted in 1918 but for almost a decade these institutions faced a struggle for real understanding of their problems on the part of those who controlled accrediting and who in most cases had little knowledge of education for prospective public school teachers.

The junior colleges, even though their conversion in some cases from weak four year colleges was fostered by the enforcement of standards of some regional associations, faced similar difficulties of recognition. Not only did they encounter delay in inclusion of their representatives on the boards and commissions of the associations, but for some time they were expected to meet requirements which were in many cases artificial adaptations of the standards for four year colleges. This same issue of control of the organizations themselves has been the basis for the continued non-admission to full voting membership in the Western College Association of the junior colleges in California, which outnumber the senior institutions in the state.

REVISION OF STANDARDS

In all societies the struggle for control is ever present, and in democratic societies the privilege of publicly expressing disagreement and contention is a well guarded one. In accrediting, this privilege has been exercised no more thoroughly and consistently than over the question of standards or requirements for accreditation. Unfortunately similar thoroughness and consistency have not prevailed over the actual review and analysis of the standards themselves. After much preliminary criticism the one massive attack on this issue was conducted by the North Central Association in the early 1930's at the cost of almost a quarter of a million dollars with the involvement of scores, even hundreds, of individuals.

The old standards, appropriate for one era, were based upon specific minimum requirements for such factors as endowment, size of library, number of academic departments, size of classes, and credit hours for graduation. The constriction of these standards was forcing leaders such as Walter A. Jessup, president of the State University of Iowa and later president of the Carnegie Corporation of New York, to proclaim, "Let the shackles of conventional and arbitrary standards be loosened in order to free the spirit of actual accomplishments on higher levels." [19] Also, standards themselves were being tested and found wanting by the studies of such men as Floyd W. Reeves of the University of Kentucky and the University of Chicago and H. H. Remmers of Purdue University. When members of the commission responsible for accrediting higher institutions in the North Central Association in 1928 "frankly admitted the inadequacy of the present standards as measures of the real worth of colleges," [20] it was then possible for the extensive study of the North Central Association to be undertaken. When it was completed in

[19] Jessup (116).   [20] North Central Association (157), 3 (June 1928), p. 9.

1934, Henry M. Wriston, a president of the association, confidently reported that it now "becomes less and less a policing body and more and more an organization designed to encourage, to stimulate, and to evaluate." [21] In adopting the principle that "an institution will be judged in terms of the purposes it seeks to serve" and on "the basis of the total pattern it presents as an institution of higher education," [22] the North Central not only abolished the old outdated standards but it evolved a radical approach by initiating a new, additional purpose of accrediting, that of providing external stimulation to institutions for their continual growth and improvement.

Partially because this new approach was such a radical departure from the old, partially because innumerable individuals and groups in accrediting were involved, partially because much time was required to convince people of the need for basic changes despite the many former criticisms—for these and other reasons, an effective method of providing a truly stimulating influence for institutional self-improvement was not devised until the Middle States Association after the second World War adopted a schedule for re-visits to all its member institutions on a ten year cycle. This new schedule involved a further revision in standards, a self-survey report by the institution, a larger number of more adequately qualified examiners, and the coordination of examiners from the appropriate professional and state accrediting agencies into a single team of visitors. With the increasing use of the pattern which included both an institutional self-survey and a team of qualified institutional inspectors, stimulation for college and university improvement was practiced more widely as a major purpose of regional accreditation. Unfortunately, however, the accomplishments in this respect among the six regional associations have shown almost as much

[21] Wriston (226).   [22] North Central Association (156).

diversity as exists among the colleges and universities themselves.[23]

MAJOR PURPOSES OF ACCREDITATION

Despite marked diversities among the regional associations they all share in common four major purposes of accreditation. Admissions and the maintenance of minimum academic standards were the two initial problems which regional accrediting was devised to meet. With changing conditions in recent years, these have receded in relative importance. As proportionately more colleges and universities have been accredited—that is, accepted into membership of the regional associations—increasing emphasis has been placed on the third purpose, that of stimulating institutional self-improvement.

The fourth major purpose of regional accrediting is to serve as a countervailing force to the many external and some internal pressures that are continually being exerted on our educational institutions. As the importance of college education for vocational, economic, and social reasons has grown, as the number of individuals enrolled in higher institutions has mounted, as the institutions themselves are providing more services to and seeking more funds from different groups of individuals, colleges and universities have become a matter of increasing importance to all segments of society. In view of the political traditions and heritage of this country it is important that there be sufficiently strong forces in education itself to counterbalance those influences that could conceivably subvert a college or a university from its true goals.

In many cases the mere presence of a regional association alert to these possibilities is sufficient to serve this purpose well. When official recognition of a deleterious situation is needed, usually quiet admonition by the accrediting association is sufficient, but on other occasions public attention is required,

[23] See Note 12, p. 99.

especially when political interference is involved. State supported colleges and universities in Georgia, Kentucky, Louisiana, Mississippi and Texas have been placed on probation or dropped from membership by the Southern Association when politicians have attempted to subject educational institutions to their own ambitions.

When the North Dakota Agricultural College was dropped from membership in the North Central Association in 1938 after the State Board of Administration had removed the president and seven senior staff members with no stated cause and no hearing, the State of North Dakota filed suit against the association. Through the decision, which was sustained by the United States Circuit Court of Appeals, the right of a regional association to take such action was supported. Consequently, regional associations were granted legal support for one of the most important purposes of their present accrediting activities—protecting colleges and universities against educationally and socially harmful pressures and forces.

OBSERVATIONS

But all of the problems in accrediting by regional associations have not been solved. We still have not learned how to judge the real quality of a college or university. Even though the regional associations now place much less reliance on specific, detailed, quantitative measurements, they continue to confront institutions with prodigious criteria and voluminous questionnaires, few of which have been verified as to their reliability in distinguishing an excellent college or an outstanding university. Reliance on empirical judgment, as presently demanded, places almost unlimited responsibility on the corps of visiting evaluators and the members of the commissions in each regional association who are charged with the obligation of making not only constructive, dynamic, and far-seeing suggestions but reasonably consistent, unbiased, and sound decisions.

The North Central Association, with the aid of a four year grant from the Carnegie Corporation, initiated in 1957 a pilot leadership training program for the purpose of educating a corps of experienced evaluators. This constructive approach faces but one of the basic problems in accrediting.

In the whole history of accreditation only a single extensive attempt has been made to study the factors and the bases on which an institution should be accredited. That was in the early 1930's, at a time when higher education was less diversified, less complex, and encountering fewer dynamic changes than today. Fortunately for all higher education many individuals are convinced that the time is arriving for a new analysis of accrediting—this time on a broad cooperative basis. However, if the regional associations do not squarely face the question of the soundness of their methods and the validity of their criteria, other forces will develop and challenge the authority of the colleges and universities to evaluate themselves through their own accrediting organizations.[24]

[24] See Note 13, p. 100.

FIVE

Governmental Reformation

THE HISTORY of the interest shown by both the federal and the state governments in the accreditation of higher education in the United States is a well documented example of the struggle over academic standards. The non-existence of an accrediting program operated by the national government can be attributed to the principles enunciated in the United States Constitution and to the American conviction that our social welfare is dependent upon education as a local responsibility. The absence of adequate state accreditation springs from a tradition of laissez-faire independence and sectarian rivalry, a fear of political interference, and a later acceptance of regional associations as the best instruments to perform what the states are legally empowered to do.

OFFICE OF EDUCATION

Although tempted on at least one occasion to serve as a

standardizing agency for the colleges and universities in the country, the United States Office of Education has, until the passage of the National Defense Education Act of 1958, confined itself primarily to summarizing educational activities and disseminating information. Created in 1867 as the Department of Education, this governmental division has been restricted through most of its varied history by limited funds. Nevertheless, it has been of substantial indirect influence in the development of higher education through studies it has made and reports it has issued.

One might have expected that the Office of Education, for many years having compiled considerable statistical information about educational institutions, would eventually be involved directly in the questions of defining and classifying colleges and universities. This involvement developed soon after Congressional authorization was granted in 1910 for the appointment of a Specialist in Higher Education and after Kendric C. Babcock, later provost and dean of the College of Liberal Arts and Sciences at the University of Illinois, was appointed to fill the position. At a time when there was growing need for a classification of colleges whose graduates were entering the graduate schools of the members of the Association of American Universities, Babcock immediately undertook the task of preparing such a list. Based on the single criterion of the success of graduates of individual colleges in master's degree programs, the list was prepared in draft form with colleges divided into four groups, of which only 17 per cent were in the first group.[1] Copies of the classifications were distributed to various deans for comments, and comments soon arrived in the form of basic criticisms.

Several of the lists inadvertently had become public knowledge and a clamor, partly from the Congress, arose to such intensity that President William Howard Taft requested that

[1] Zook (228).

the list be withheld. Not even an official request addressed to President Woodrow Wilson in 1913 by the Association of American Universities was sufficient to dislodge the classification from its assigned place of obscurity. Samuel P. Capen, a successor to Babcock as Specialist in Higher Education, later commented that "the bureau learned that there are no second and third and fourth class colleges; that it was an outrage and infamy so to designate institutions whose sons reflected honor on the state and the nation." [2]

In 1913 Babcock himself correctly predicted that "further efforts along this line are likely to be more or less hampered by possible political complications and pleas of special groups of institutions." [3] Never again did the United States Office of Education attempt to exercise its own judgment in evaluating and classifying educational institutions.[4] Following the 1911–1913 episode a committee representing associations of higher educational institutions recommended that the Bureau of Education, as it was then called, issue statistical reports based on information obtained from questionnaires designed by the bureau and completed by the colleges and universities themselves. This policy has been pursued consistently ever since.

Beginning in 1917 the Office of Education has issued approximately every four years a publication entitled *Accredited Higher Institutions* which includes the lists of institutions accredited by the states and the recognized regional and professional accrediting agencies. The basis for inclusion of the lists of the various agencies varied somewhat over the years until the Veterans' Readjustment Assistance Act of 1952 [5] charged the Commissioner of Education with the responsibility of publishing "a list of nationally recognized accrediting agencies and associations which he determines to be reliable authority as to

[2] Capen (39).   [3] Babcock (11).   [4] See Note 14, p. 100.   [5] P. L. 550, 82nd Congress, Sec. 253.

the quality of training offered by an educational institution." [6]
In carrying out the provisions of this act the Office of Education prepared criteria or standards which accrediting agencies
must meet in order that their lists of approved institutions may
be included in *Accredited Higher Institutions*. What is more,
it has become increasingly important that institutions be accredited and listed in this publication, since omission adversely
affects the status of a college or university and its graduates
with almost all government departments and agencies.[7] As
larger amounts of government funds have been made available
to higher education, it has become economically and vitally
necessary that an institution be accredited and that an accrediting agency be approved by the United States Commissioner
of Education.

ACCREDITATION BY THE STATES

Although at the federal level there is legal authority only
for the Commissioner of Education to recognize or approve
accrediting agencies, in most states there is legal authorization
for actual accreditation by some one of the state governmental
agencies. It may be called accepting, appraising, approving,
classifying, listing, or registering, but in any case it means some
modified pattern of accrediting. And it may be conducted by
the department of education, a state university, a special commission, an association of collegiate institutions; or it may not
be carried out at all, as frequently happens, in which case reliance is placed almost completely on the lists prepared by the
non-government accrediting agencies. But this apparently hap-
hazard, variegated pattern of state control of standards for
higher education did not bloom without attempts to transplant
the British and the European systems to this inhospitable land.

In 1876 S. S. Laws, president of the University of Missouri,
publicly proposed a federation of colleges with the state uni-

[6] United States Office of Education (214).   [7] See Note 15, p. 101.

versity granting the degrees to those who successfully passed common examinations.[8] This idea, supported some years later by the United States Commissioner of Education, W. T. Harris, was received like chaff on barren ground.

Only slightly more effective have been the suggestions that the states should exercise greater responsibility for the chartering and supervising of colleges and universities. Resolutions as early as 1897 and 1898 by the National Education Association and the North Central Association urged the states to fulfill their obligations to exercise more effective supervision over degree-granting institutions. Henry Wade Rogers, president of Northwestern University, at the National Education Association meeting in 1897 declared:

The cause of professional as well as of academic education suffers from the want of adequate State supervision. . . . This sort of thing, impossible in Europe, should be made impossible in America. Such a condition of affairs is demoralizing beyond question. The tendency of it is all in the direction of low standards. It imposes on the public a class of educational charlatans and works injury to the students whom it falsely pretends to educate.[9]

The dishonesty and fraudulence in education which Rogers implied not only existed then but exists now. The famous and profitable Oriental University which was closed some thirty-five years ago only after much publicity and legal action is not the only example of the sordid practice of selling degrees in an unethical and frequently illegal manner. Even though there is general ignorance of this fact, similar institutions exist today, and in large numbers.[10] In California alone a recent study by a subcommittee of the State Assembly reported there were at least fifty such organizations selling degrees with sub-standard requirements, that "in most cases, the schools issuing the degree were bona fide California corporations, authorized

[8] See Note 16, p. 101.   [9] Harris (96), 1897-98, Vol. 2, p. 1463.   [10] See Note 17, p. 101.

by the Secretary of State, under sections of the Education code," and that the problem has been increasing in recent years.[11] Not only is this a matter of national importance; it is an issue of profound gravity in our international relations. A former trial attorney for the Federal Trade Commission testified only a few years past that "practically all of these unsavory institutions have a substantial, and sometimes exclusive, enrollment of foreign students," and "this puts a considerable strain on friendly relations with foreign countries." [12]

LAXITY OF STATE GOVERNMENTS

As recently as 1954 sixteen states required no charter or license for an educational institution to operate and at least seventeen states lacked adequate laws to authorize the closing of fraudulent schools or diploma mills.[13] Educators have declared that state legislatures lack the interest and the will to enact appropriate legislation, and in turn legislators have admonished the educators by saying that "we can never have satisfactory educational legislation ... till the educationists, all together, really want what they think they want, make up their minds to pay the price in time and effort and courage, and go out and get it." [14] For some the price has implied a threat to academic freedom and for others it has implied an even more important threat—control of non-tax supported institutions by state departments of education or by state universities. The competition that has persisted for almost two centuries among the colleges and later among the universities of this country has been a fundamental reason why strong state control has been accepted in only one or two states.

Another attempt to encourage the states to assume greater responsibility for the supervision of higher education was made when the National Council of Chief State School Officers in

[11] California, Assembly of (36), pp. 7-8; also, see Note 18, p. 102.
[12] Penche (164).   [13] Edmonson (74).   [14] Churchill (47).

1937 formally requested the United States Office of Education "to recommend standards which may be used by the departments of education in the several States for the accreditation of post-secondary institutions." [15] The report which was prepared in response to this request specifically recommended that in place of the regional associations all the states do the accrediting. The reaction to this suggestion was either opposition or indifference. Opposition was expressed on the grounds that there might be political interference with the institutions and that the states presented too many small geographical divisions for reasonable comparability in accrediting. Indifference permeated the chief state school officers when they realized that "it would be hard enough to develop standards for one state without thinking of standards that would apply within all states." [16] Today opposition and indifference continue to prevail in most states despite the successful and contrasting example of New York.

NEW YORK BOARD OF REGENTS

As the oldest continuous state educational administrative agency in the United States, the University of the State of New York has increased its influence and control since its creation in the eighteenth century. The university, governed by the Board of Regents and directed by the State Commissioner of Education and several thousand subordinates, consists of all the educational corporations in the state. Its powers, which are similar to those of a ministry of education in a foreign country, are so broad that "no privately controlled institution is permitted to confer degrees, transact any business, or in any way assume the name of college or university without first obtaining written permission from the Regents under their seal." [17] In fact, the Board of Regents may suspend the charter of any

15 Kelly (121); also, see Note 19, p. 102. 16 See Note 20, p. 102. 17 McNeely (134), p. 49.

educational institution if in its judgment an institution fails to comply with the state regulations, and it may even appoint the chief executive officer of an institution if the position has remained unfilled for more than a year without proper excuse. While rules and regulations of this type, together with fine leadership, have helped to maintain relatively high educational standards in the State of New York, the authority of the Board of Regents over professional registration or licensure has had its influence on education both throughout the United States and in foreign countries.

The authority to license individuals to practice a profession was first assigned to the Board of Regents in the 1870's when it was empowered to examine and license medical doctors as a protection for the public welfare. Over the intervening years as the number of different professions has grown, the authority of licensure has been correspondingly increased for the Regents. Under their regulations as many as eighteen thousand professional candidates have been examined in a single year, and for a candidate to be eligible to take a professional examination his professional, and in some cases, pre-professional program of studies must be accredited, or registered as it is called in New York, in accordance with the Regents' regulations. This registration of curriculums is not limited to institutions in New York but applies equally to colleges and universities in any part of the world—in fact, wherever the candidate may have studied.[18] Through this power of requiring not merely the passing of a licensure examination but also the accreditation of the specific curriculum which the candidate studies, no matter in what institution or where it is located, the Board of Regents of the University of the State of New York has indeed become a powerful force in the external control of higher education.

Quite incongruous is the practice in many other states of

18 See Note 21, p. 102.

granting charters to educational institutions in an almost profligate manner and at the same time requiring that candidates for a profession be graduated from accredited colleges and universities in order to be eligible to take the qualifying licensure examinations. And yet all states, in order to protect the public, require licensure in many professions, and most states include regulations as to the quality of previous education by using such terms as accredited, approved, listed, or registered.[19] In practically all the states, the responsibility is officially assigned to a board of licensing examiners, usually composed of members of the appropriate profession; and with a few exceptions, such as New York State, reliance is placed upon the national professional agency to prepare the list of accredited institutions. It is this authority of accrediting, delegated by the states as a part of their licensing procedure, that makes some of the national professional accrediting agencies extremely powerful forces in the struggle over standards for higher education in the United States.

OBSERVATIONS

After years of active and intense participation in government at both the federal and state levels, Gifford Pinchot, then governor of Pennsylvania, spoke at the Governors' Conference in 1926 on "The State, the Nation and the People's Needs." With the enthusiasm of one of the early advocates for conservation of natural resources he correctly observed the history of political developments in the United States. Not merely reflecting on past and current history but anticipating developments of the coming decades, Pinchot stated:

If the people need action and a township fails to supply it, the county naturally steps in; if the county fails, the state steps in; if the state fails, the Nation steps in. Many thing are being done to-

19 See Note 22, p. 102.

day by the Nation simply because the States, for whatever reasons, have failed to give the people what they properly require.[20]

This observation applies not only to natural resources or to economic resources; it applies equally well to educational resources.

One hundred years ago when the individual colleges and the states were not providing education adequate for the needs of the people, the Federal Congress passed the land-grant college act which practically revolutionized higher education in the United States. One might logically conclude that if the states, for whatever reasons, do not now provide for the people and the nation adequate protection against fraudulence and inadequate standards in education, the Federal Congress again will find a way to act where the states have failed. Burgeoning pressures from increasing college age populations provide economic inducements for the operation of institutions with inadequate, even dishonest, standards. This type of institution the people now will not accept and the nation can no longer afford. Consequently, increased and active governmental interest in academic standards may confidently be predicted.

[20] Pinchot (169).

SIX

Professional Reformation

THE UNFINISHED picture of accrediting portrayed so far may look to the uninitiated as an impressionistic painting would have appeared to Pericles. If the continental or British forms of external control of standards in higher education are compared to the classical lines of a Greek temple, one can liken accreditation to a contemporary piece of abstract art. It takes time as well as interest to understand both abstract art and accreditation, and especially so with the latter when one includes the accrediting of professional programs of study. John D. Millett, now president of Miami University, has written: "Professional accrediting is one of the knottiest administrative and financial problems of higher education." [1]

[1] Millett (137), p. 21.

55

PROFESSIONAL DEVELOPMENTS

Professional accrediting, most of which is supported indirectly by licensure laws in the various states, is intimately related to the desires of individuals to attain a high vocational status. When individuals in a particular group discover that they are using a common body of knowledge which has been developed and is identifiable and communicable through an intellectual process of higher education, inevitably they band together to form a professional association. Not only do they aim to create an organization which will foster research, advance learning in the profession, and improve service to the public, but they develop an impelling motive to raise individual status by restricting admission to the profession—sometimes with more emphasis on the interests of the practitioners than on the public welfare.

The issue of control over admission is extremely important to any profession. This is especially true in the formative stages of a profession as it fights for recognition and struggles against the superior attitude of the established professions. For this reason, as well as for the interests of the public, almost all professions strive for restrictions of admission through state licensure laws and through their own accreditation of the colleges and universities which offer the programs of study leading to the particular professions.

With the rapid increase in the number of professions the situation has become not just abstract, but complex and confusing. Until the nineteenth century it was possible to say:

> The learned professions, all agree,
> Are physic, law, and divinity.[2]

But no longer. Now there are scores of professions, about thirty of which are actively doing accrediting on a national

[2] Smith (200), p. 150.

scale while others enviously wish they could pursue this activity which medicine initiated so successfully in 1904. The dramatic improvement in medical education, following the introduction of accrediting and the subsequent famous report of Abraham Flexner in 1910, set a precedent which many other professions have attempted to follow.[3] Medicine deserves this recognition because conditions in its early schools and colleges were disgraceful and socially harmful.

REFORM IN MEDICAL EDUCATION

Apprentice training, the accepted method of professional education in the early nineteenth century, gave way partially to empirical teaching by practitioners who banded together to organize privately owned and operated medical schools. At the time the American Medical Association was created in 1847 the doctor of medicine degree was being awarded for less than six months of study plus some apprenticeship, and standards in admission requirements were practically nonexistent. Because the demand for doctors and the anticipation of personal profits were so great, the number of medical schools increased until 1906 when there were one hundred and sixty-two.[4] In writing of all professional education of that time, Lloyd E. Blauch, recent United States Assistant Commissioner for Higher Education, has stated:

. . . with notable exceptions, education for the professions near the close of the nineteenth century was in a sad state. Most of the professional schools were wretchedly housed and almost never in quarters designed for the needs of the professional instruction. Their only income was from student fees, which covered the costs of operation and provided a profit for the owner. The entrance requirements were few and low. The majority of the students could not have been admitted to colleges requiring entrance tests. The courses were almost entirely didactic.[5]

[3] See Note 23, p. 103.   [4] Fishbein (80).   [5] Blauch (21), p. 11.

In view of these conditions it is no surprise that many of the operators of the schools would object to Flexner's investigation and cause him to include in his report: "A considerable number of colleges and universities take the unfortunate position that they are private institutions and that the public is entitled to only such knowledge of their operations as they choose to communicate." [6] But the spirit of reform was in the air and the age of the muckrakers was at hand. Medical education and all professional education was bound to feel this influence.

Acceptance of the idea that medical education needed drastic improvement spread slowly at first. The reform of the Harvard Medical School in 1871, the opening of the influential Johns Hopkins Medical School in 1893, the organization of the Association of American Medical Colleges in 1890 could not alone overcome resistance to change on the part of the majority of schools and on the part of the large numbers of practitioners who thought their training would thereby be questioned. Although the Council on Medical Education of the American Medical Association did publish its first list of classified schools in 1906–1907 it was primarily publicity from the Flexner Report that stimulated the closing of deficient schools so that by 1920 there was a reduction to eighty-five, almost all of which by this time were associated with universities.[7] It truly could be said that the progress of medical education was "the most outstanding single feature in the history of professional education in the United States during this period," [8] and it can also be claimed that accrediting had much to do with this progress.

REFORM IN LEGAL EDUCATION

The struggle over standards in legal education took place in a manner similar to that in medicine though progress was

[6] Flexner (81), Introduction.   [7] Allen (4), p. 16.   [8] Babcock (14).

slower and complete victory has not yet been attained. For years recommendations, reports, and resolutions regarding training for and admission to the bar were presented at the meetings of the American Bar Association, organized in 1878; but for some time general interest could not be engendered among the majority of its members, many of whom had studied law in the Abraham Lincoln tradition. Not for a long time was the public ready for a change from "the frontier idea which was expressed in the Constitution of Indiana in 1851— 'Every person of good moral character, being a voter, shall be entitled to admission to practice law in all courts of justice.' " [9]

Repeated emphasis on the need for improved legal education finally led to an eight year study financed by the Carnegie Foundation and a report in 1921 by a special committee of which Elihu Root served as chairman. This report included recommendations that college work of at least two years should precede admission to law school, graduation from which should be one of the requirements for admission to the bar, and that a list of law schools which comply with American Bar Association's standards should be made public.[10] From that date, accrediting by the American Bar Association has been a potent influence for the improvement of law schools, the majority of which are now divisions of universities, although the force behind these requirements is mitigated by the fact that not all states, even now, require graduation from an accredited school of law for admission to the bar.

The frontier spirit continues to exert its influence in some areas of the country when it comes to the question of permission to practice law. In addition, some members of the Council of Legal Education and Admissions to the Bar, which is the committee entrusted by the American Bar Association with the responsibility of presenting recommendations on the accreditation of law schools, believe that much further progress

[9] Pound (172), p. 8.   [10] See Note 24, p. 103.

needs to be made. This attitude is reflected in their criticism of those schools of law that are parts of universities where considerably more interest seems to be concentrated on the amount of income produced by the law schools than in the requisite steps necessary to provide strong legal education. And so the struggle over standards continues.[11]

OTHER PROFESSIONS

Although the ancient and honored professions of medicine and law were the first to develop accreditation as a means of raising educational standards in their respective fields of study, they soon were not alone in this endeavor. Landscape architecture, library science, music, nursing, optometry, teacher education, and collegiate business education were some of the fields in which accrediting was begun before the end of the 1920's, to be followed in the 1930's by chemistry, dentistry, engineering, forestry, pharmacy, social work, theology, and veterinary medicine, and by others in the 1940's.[12] The example of medicine and law had affected other academic specialties at a time when conditions were ripe for the spread of this native method of controlling standards in higher education.

The development of industry and communication and the expanding population and urbanization of the country were accompanied by increasing wealth which could support not only the demand for more professional people but the educational facilities required in the transmission of new knowledge and recently discovered techniques. With stimulus from the land-grant college act and encouragement by professions which wished to destroy the blight of proprietary schools, many colleges and universities, in contrast to the continental or British practices, competed with each other by adding professional schools beyond their resources to support them.

[11] See Note 25, p. 103.   [12] See Note 26, p. 103.

The financial depression of the 1930's saw educational budgets being reduced and a consequent increase in accrediting by professional groups, which are always concerned with the effect of reduced appropriations on their schools.

As enrollment in the graduate schools doubled almost every decade, professionalism developed in the intellectual life of the campuses. Organizations of those engaged in the various academic specialties sought and gained grants from philanthropic foundations to support studies which in many cases concluded with recommendations that they undertake accrediting as a means of maintaining the standards proposed in the reports. The precedent for this type of approach undoubtedly was set by the Carnegie Foundation for the Advancement of Teaching which has been called "the most startling and epoch making force for the improvement of professional education." [13] At least twelve studies financed by the Carnegie Foundation or the Carnegie Corporation culminated in or gave strong support to accrediting of professional fields of study.[14]

Concomitant with the increase in professionalism has been a growth of departmentalization of college and university faculties. Not limited to large universities, where for administrative reasons alone separation of the faculty into divisions has become a necessity, departmentalization is now an accepted practice even among the smallest colleges. As a result of the growing size of institutions and the specialization and departmentalization of faculties, professors frequently find more responsive relationships and greater agreement with those in the same field of study on other campuses than with their fellow faculty members in different fields on the same campus.

On a college campus "there is a constant tug and haul of competing forces, a constant struggle for influence and prestige." [15] This struggle can often be won by the group which

[13] Brubacher and Rudy (31), p. 205. [14] See Note 27, p. 104. [15] Abbott (1), p. 63.

is supported by a national professional organization, especially if that organization is an accrediting agency, as the American Chemical Society which found accrediting to be "the best means of increasing the professional standing of chemists." [16] Professors in fields as diverse as agriculture, English composition and communication, home economics, physical education, and theater arts, have longingly envied the chemists and their powerful organization which succeeded, over heavy opposition from university administrators, in embarking on a program of accrediting.

The competition among groups with the interplay of differing points of view has been a never ending struggle through the ebb and flow of history. Conflicts among nations and rivalries between political parties are natural manifestations in the difficult art of human relations as personal and group aspirations are translated into action. These same struggles and jealousies are found among professional groups—whether they are demanding higher standards and more funds, at the indirect expense of other programs of study; whether they are seeking improved status relative to another profession, as the clinical psychologists versus the psychiatrists, or the nurses versus the doctors; or whether they are competing for control of a curriculum, as the music educators and the teacher educators have argued over music education, or the engineers and the military have argued over military and naval science. The multiplication of these professional associations, like the new nations of contemporary Asia and Africa, grows apace as some splinter off from parent groups and others are born anew. Fortunately once in awhile there is a coalescence when one agency is created by combining a number of competing organizations, as has happened in journalism, nursing, and social work; but these transformations do not result without some strain and stress over the question of control.

[16] Noyes (159).

STRUGGLES OVER STANDARDS IN TEACHER EDUCATION

In the entire history of accreditation probably the most intense, bitter, and widespread struggle developed over the question of accrediting programs of study in teacher education. Conditions during the earliest days of labor negotiations could hardly have aroused more passion and unreasonableness than was expressed by the extremists over this issue. As in the case of the labor movement, the development of teacher education had a long historical background. Imported from Europe, the idea of schools devoted only to the preparation of teachers took root in this country when the first private normal school was established at Concord, Vermont in 1823, soon followed in the 1830's by the first public normal schools. With an expanding population and a corresponding increase in school enrollments, in time supported by compulsory school attendance laws, the demand for teachers, on which the liberal arts colleges turned their backs, encouraged the growth of normal schools. Socially ostracized by the liberal arts colleges, these schools formed their own organization in 1855 prior to their association with the Department of Normal Schools of the National Education Association in 1870, and ever since have waged a battle for academic acceptance. Through a tortuous course, the normal schools and their successors, the state teachers colleges, first attempted to raise standards by themselves and later, with the growth of the regional associations, sought understanding and adequate recognition from these accrediting associations which were then controlled by the liberal arts colleges and universities.

The path to acceptance was strewn with many hurdles. Inertia, prejudice, deep seated convictions, and profound philosophical differences played their part. But competition for students also developed as an important factor when liberal arts colleges and universities added departments and schools of education in a belated recognition of the facts that the enormous school population required teachers and that these teachers needed to know something about teaching as well as what to teach. Although inclusion of a department of education on a liberal arts campus might assist in the enrollment of students, it did not mean academic acceptance of the professors of education or respectability for the subjects they taught. The great educational schism which started in the early nineteenth century continued as the liberal arts faculties and the teacher education faculties largely went their separate ways— the liberal arts faculties unaware of and unconcerned with the overburdening social demands being saddled on the elementary and secondary schools by public needs and pressures, and the teacher education faculties largely impatient with the emphasis on scholarly and academic accomplishment as they became engrossed in the operational problems of the public schools.

For years the differences between these two groups smoldered, until teacher educationists proposed in the late 1940's the creation of a national agency to accredit *all* programs of teacher education. Since the 1920's the American Association of Colleges for Teacher Education and its predecessor organizations had been accrediting the schools and colleges of education and only rarely a program offered by a liberal arts college. When the National Council for Accreditation of Teacher Education was organized in 1952 the smoldering broke into a conflagration. The liberal arts people, although unorganized, made plain their opposition—first to the extension of professional accrediting into an area which they insisted could be adequately served by the regional associations, second to the acceptance of the argument that teaching is a profession like medicine, law, or nursing, and third to the relationship of the certification of teachers with the accrediting of liberal arts colleges by a national professional teacher education accrediting agency.[17] But their most weighty barrage was concentrated on the control of this new agency, whose governing council included representatives of schools of education, public school teachers, school boards, chief state school officers, and directors of state certification. And it was this last point on which the compromise finally turned. Representatives of liberal arts interests were included on a revised board of control with a reduced representation of the other groups. The support behind this professional accrediting drive was so strong that the disorganized opposing forces could not stem the tide of the united groups' insistence on the need to employ accreditation as a means of raising the standards for teacher education and of improving the professional status of teachers.

OBSERVATIONS

Throughout the entire accrediting movement the question of influence or control has been a paramount issue. In professional accrediting this is apparent in two ways: in the composition of the board responsible for accreditation and in the demands presented to the institutions. The committees responsible for professional accrediting vary considerably in their membership. Some comprise only practitioners; some, only representatives of the professional schools; some, a combination of both; and others, a combination of both plus representatives of state licensing officials.[18] But in only two cases, pharmacy and teacher education, are representatives of the central administrations of colleges and universities intentionally included.

Students of professional education have observed that even though all professions are anxious to have and many are insistent upon having their schools affiliated with universities, the relationship desired is one of autonomy.[19] All too frequently "there is an almost total lack of awareness of the need

[17] See Note 28, p. 104.   [18] See Note 29, p. 104.   [19] See Note 30, p. 104.

for integration of a professional school into the organizational framework of a larger institution of which it may be a part and for the coordination necessary in problems of administration." [20] Insistence upon a separate school with a dean reporting to the president or vice president of the university, regardless of the best administrative practice for the particular institution, is a common example of this aspiration for autonomy.

A partial answer to this problem would be to have some representation of the central administrations on all commissions and committees responsible for accrediting professional programs of study. If this practice were widely adopted, at least there would be increased mutual understanding between the professions and the administrators of higher institutions, even though an end could not be expected to the ever-recurrent and natural desire of professional groups to seek academic identity and independence.[21]

In facing the future we may confidently expect that the number of professions and semi-professions will continue to increase and that each will be based on programs of education provided by colleges and universities. However, we cannot so confidently expect to provide the correct answer to the question—how do we face the demand of more professions wishing to undertake accreditation? A continued increase in the number of professional accrediting agencies would encourage faster subdivision of university faculties and fragmentation of college curriculums, and also would reduce educational freedom of action even further.[22] The prospect of this development has given support to the counter-reformation in accrediting, a movement which has been led by the larger universities in which most of the professional programs are concentrated.[23]

[20] Witmer (224), p. 107. [21] See Note 31, p. 105. [22] See Note 32, p. 105.
[23] See Note 33, p. 105.

SEVEN

Counter-Reformation

IN THE seventeenth century Sir Isaac Newton discovered that for every action in the field of physical motion there is an equal and opposite reaction. In the twentieth century not one but many have discovered that for every extension of accrediting there develops an opposite, but not necessarily equal, reaction—and that this reaction is often more emotional than physical, and not always constant. The counter-reformation movement in accrediting, though not led by the Association of American Universities, can be appreciated by reviewing how this august organization became one of the most influential accrediting agencies only to repudiate at a later date both its own activities and those of all other accrediting agencies.

ASSOCIATION OF AMERICAN UNIVERSITIES

The unstable conditions in the academic world of the

United States at the beginning of this century affected not merely the secondary schools and colleges but also the graduate schools, which then were still in their formative stage of development. Graduate students themselves, concerned for recognition of their degrees, had presented in 1893 and again in 1896 formal resolutions through the Federation of Graduate Clubs to the governing boards of the universities urging universal acceptance of standards. By 1900 the presidents of California, Chicago, Columbia, Harvard, and Johns Hopkins universities formally recognized the need for common action and addressed a letter to the presidents of a select number of universities inviting them to a conference, the deliberations of which, they predicted, would

(1) result in a greater uniformity of the conditions under which students may become candidates for higher degrees in different American universities, thereby solving the question of migration, which has become an important issue with the Federation of Graduate Clubs; (2) raise the opinion entertained abroad of our own Doctor's degree; and (3) raise the standard of our own weaker institutions.[1]

At a time when German universities were the cynosure of most graduate students it was inevitable that these centers of learning and research would have a marked influence on the formation and development of the Association of American Universities; and that they had.

Dubious of the standards maintained in most American educational institutions, the University of Berlin in 1904 resolved its dilemma by deciding that "in order to have graduate work pursued at an American university credited by this faculty . . . the candidate must have taken his graduate work at one of the institutions represented in the Association of American Universities."[2] This action gave evidence of the position of re-

[1] Association of American Universities (9), 1901, p. 11. [2] Association of American Universities (9), 1905.

spect which the association had attained even at that time and it also placed before this organization an issue which it had to face.

Charles W. Eliot, no one to shirk a responsibility, served as chairman of a Special Committee on Aims and Scope of the association which reported in 1908 that "it is the duty of this Association either to standardize American universities, and then justify the confidence which foreign governments repose in them, or to notify those governments that there are American universities outside this Association whose work and standing are not inferior to universities now members of the Association." [3] Recognizing the injustice being done those institutions which were not members of the Association of American Universities, the special committee concluded its report with the recommendation that "a committee for the standardization of American colleges" be appointed.

In the spirit of the times when standardization was a necessity, when definitions for such terms as department, course, college, and school were required, when the members realized that leadership was needed, the association unanimously approved the special committee report in 1909 and laid the basis for its eventual accreditation of colleges. It was not an easy task; the first list was delayed to allow sufficient time to consider how to proceed and to ascertain that the classification prepared by Kendric C. Babcock in the United States Office of Education would not be released. [4] When finally issued in 1914 this first list included the names of one hundred and nineteen institutions, comprising the Association's membership of twenty-two, the institutions on the approved list of the Carnegie Foundation, and those institutions which would have qualified for the Carnegie list if they had not been sectarian in control.

Now launched as an accrediting agency, the Association of

[3] Association of American Universities (9), 1908. [4] See Chapter 5, pp. 46-47.

American Universities, occasionally called the Ph.D. Trust,[5] devoted much time at its annual meetings to the consideration of requests from additional colleges wishing to be included on the approved list. The Committee on Classification, having grown dissatisfied with the method of rating colleges on the basis of the success of their graduates in graduate schools, proposed in 1923 the inauguration of a system of personal visits to the applying colleges which would be financed by inspection fees, later increased, and a grant from the Carnegie Foundation. This new program involved the finances and absorbed the attention of the association to such an extent that interest on the part of the university presidents waned and their attendance at meetings became exceedingly irregular. Continued attention to accreditation at each annual meeting led to a revolt in 1948, and this revolt, which could have been called a trust-busting movement, served as the catalyst for the counter-reformation in accrediting which reached its high water mark in the early 1950's.

JOINT COMMITTEE ON ACCREDITING

While occasional outbursts of opposition to accrediting were heard at the meetings of the Association of American Universities, the National Association of State Universities, whose sessions were attended only by the university presidents, was the first organization to express deep concern over the increase in number and variety of standardizing agencies. This alarm took the form of an authorization for a special study which was completed in 1926 by Fred J. Kelly, then Dean of Administration at the University of Minnesota and later, Chief of the Division of Higher Education in the United States Office of Education. The study was the first thorough analysis to be undertaken of accrediting, an activity in higher education which was not well understood then and seems to

[5] MacLean (128).

be comprehended no more readily now. The final report included a review of all the accrediting agencies and concluded with the following unanswered questions:

Should not standardizing agencies limit their standardizing activities to the making of sets of definitions which incorporate the present opinions of the membership, and to marshaling such data as they can in support of their opinions, leaving to the legally constituted authorities in each state the task of enforcing requirements?

Should there not be some educational council which represents all phases of education, for the purpose of examining these sets of definitions, and of giving its reactions to them in the light of a broader, more general conception of education? [6]

As so often happens in large organizations, the attention of the association's members was soon attracted to other matters. The National Association of State Universities made no attempt to answer these or any other questions related to accrediting until exasperation led in 1938 to the formation of the Joint Committee on Accrediting. This committee represented a cooperative attack by the National Association of State Universities and the American Association of Land-Grant Colleges and State Universities against all accrediting, particularly accrediting of professional fields of study.

AMERICAN COUNCIL ON EDUCATION

Meanwhile, the American Council on Education, organized during the First World War to represent all segments of higher education, developed an immediate interest in accrediting and appointed a Committee on College Standards which was to become the successor to the National Conference Committee on Standards of Colleges and Secondary Schools.[7] The new committee, which was the first in a series of American Council committees concerned with accrediting, was "com-

[6] Kelly (119). [7] See Chapter 4, pp. 34-35.

posed of representatives of the principal standardizing bodies" who were appointed "to bring about a greater uniformity of procedures among the principal agencies now engaged in defining college standards." [8] Their early deliberations brought immediate success in their attempts to develop some uniformity as various accrediting agencies agreed to adopt the standards proposed by the committee for the major types of institutions. But the initial success of this committee was not equaled in the accomplishments of its later activities or those of its successor committees. As an organization created to represent all higher education, the American Council on Education found itself in a difficult position of cross-fire as individual expressions of protest against accrediting led to an organized clamor of resistance in the late 1930's, culminating in a crescendo of opposition in the early 1950's.

In a conference on accrediting sponsored by the council in 1939, Samuel P. Capen, its first president, thundered forth in his peroration of condemnation, "Seven Devils in Exchange for One," the resounding echoes of which limited attention to the equally significant speech—"Objectionable Practices of Accrediting Agencies"—presented by John J. Tigert, then president of the University of Florida and chairman of the Joint Committee on Accrediting, and former United States Commissioner of Education. Tigert criticized the accrediting agencies for being too numerous, for invading the rights of institutions and destroying institutional freedom, for encouraging uniformity and restricting experimentation, for assessing excessive costs, for demanding too much duplication of effort,[9] for sometimes considering matters irrelevant to accrediting, for employing outmoded standards, and for developing a guild system or trade unionist attitude. He then outlined the intentions of the Joint Committee on Accrediting formed the

[8] *Educational Record*, 1 (January, 1920), p. 32; also, see Note 34, p. 105.
[9] See Note 35, p. 106.

previous year: to pass on any new agencies trying to start accrediting, to prepare an approved list of accrediting agencies, to work eventually towards the elimination of some, to foster simplification in procedures and a reduction in duplication, to end any dictation by groups outside the educational field, and to restore a proper responsibility to the states and the institutions.

In undertaking this first organized attack against the excesses of accreditation, the Joint Committee, under the chairmanship of Tigert, met with representatives of accrediting agencies and then advised the presidents of the state universities and of the land-grant colleges which of these organizations should be added to their approved list. Later augmented by representatives of the Association of Urban Universities and of the Association of American Universities, even though the latter was still an active accrediting agency itself, the Joint Committee continued its endeavors to limit the spread of accrediting and to restrict the influence of these agencies, in what Tigert called "a very difficult problem to attack." [10] In contrast to the more aggressive approach of the committee of university presidents, the American Council on Education continued its interest by fostering another conference in 1940 prior to which Alfred Z. Reed of the Carnegie Foundation had prepared a study of accrediting in which he commented:

The task can be performed well, or it can be performed badly, but since it meets a genuine social need, it avails nothing to complain that it is never done so well as we should like. The efforts of all interested parties should be directed, instead, toward trying to have what must be done, done better.[11]

In compliance with this advice the conference included among its actions a recommendation that the American Council Committee on the Study of Accrediting Procedures

[10] National Association of State Universities (141), 1939. [11] Reed (179), pp. 33-34.

try to develop a master questionnaire or schedule which all the accrediting agencies might use. This onerous and complicated task, though undertaken forthwith, was soon bogged down to a standstill by insufficient funds and by the growing problems of the Second World War which were pressing for more immediate attention than the bothersome issues of accrediting. During these years of military engagement the accrediting agencies also were absorbed by other demands so that their activities became relatively less irksome to the college and university presidents; but this was only a passing phase. The end of the war unleashed a pent-up urge to increase the number of professional accrediting agencies, at the very time when renewed doubts as to the efficacy of accrediting were being widely expressed—no more positively than by some of the presidents whose institutions were leading members of the Association of American Universities.

END OF AAU ACCREDITING

An attempt in 1945 and 1946 to extend accrediting by the Association of American Universities into graduate study not only went down to defeat but served as a prelude for a successful attack two years later against all accrediting by the association. A group of determined opponents, who could well have resurrected the appropriate battle cry, "Stand fast, . . . brethren, in the liberty wherewith we are made free and be not entangled with any yoke of bondage," [12] based their arguments not on emotional appeals but on the conviction that accreditation as conducted by the association was not being done well and might be of more harm than good, and that it no longer was a factor of importance in deciding admission to graduate work. In fact, studies were proving that "students from institutions accredited and not accredited by AAU" were doing "almost equally well in graduate

[12] Winship (223).

schools." [13] Despite protests both within and without the association, the vote was overwhelmingly in favor of a drastic change in the organization and the discontinuation of all accrediting as of October 1948. In their haste to register disapproval, even distaste, for accrediting, the leaders of this rebellion gave no heed to the immediate consequences of their momentous decision and provided no assistance to those who had over the years placed increased reliance on the AAU list as the only roster of superior institutions in the United States. The spirit of revolt and the desire to attack all accrediting permeated the new leadership of the association. [14]

While the Association of American Universities divested itself of an unwieldy burden when it discontinued its accrediting procedures, other organizations were suddenly confronted with the dilemma of discovering adequate substitutes. The American Association of University Women and Phi Beta Kappa solved their problems merely by increasing the quasi-accrediting activities which they had been conducting for some years. Foreign governments and institutions, in not the same fortunate position, found no satisfactory answer to their need for a list of the better colleges and universities in this country. [15] The Southern Association adopted a resolution urging AAU to continue its accreditation until some other agency could be created to assume the responsibility; and the American Council on Education convened another conference in 1949 entitled "The Accrediting Agencies Face Their Common Problems." [16]

Attended by representatives of many educational organizations, including most accrediting agencies, the conference recommended that a thorough study by the American Council be undertaken of most all phases of accreditation:

[13] Edwards (75).   [14] See Note 36, p. 106.   [15] See Note 37, p. 106.
[16] Brumbaugh (32).

The extent to which accrediting standards are written into federal and state laws and regulations; the control exercised over higher institutions by various agencies and groups; the effects of accreditation, good or bad, on higher institutions; the extent to which examinations could be used in the process of accreditation; a further analysis of the duplication of information requested by accrediting agencies; an analysis of the policies and criteria employed by the regional accrediting associations for the purpose of identifying points of agreement and variation.[17]

Since no foundation grants were ever made available for this ambitious study or for any parts of it, the only tangible accomplishment of the conference was the creation of the National Committee of Regional Accrediting Agencies whose chief aim was to include a greater degree of uniformity and cooperation among all accrediting agencies. Although this committee has annually published a list of regionally accredited institutions and has provided an opportunity each year for personal discussions among the two representatives from each regional association, it has had limited influence and according to one of its members it "has not lived up to its earlier promise."[18]

NATIONAL COMMISSION ON ACCREDITING

The overshadowing event of this time was the formation of the National Commission on Accrediting in 1949 and its subsequent aggressive attack on professional accrediting agencies. Perceiving no indications that the regional associations were cooperating with the Joint Committee and provoked by "the apparent abuses and unhealthy restraints"[19] of accrediting, the presidents of the land-grant colleges, the liberal arts colleges, state universities, private universities, and urban universities enlarged the Joint Committee and transformed it into the National Commission under the vigorous and dynamic leadership of Reuben G. Gustavson, then chancellor of the

[17] Zook (230), 1950.   [18] Nyquist (160).   [19] Hazen (98).

University of Nebraska and chairman of the Joint Committee.[20] Speaking for the presidents on different occasions Gustavson stated, "The immediate reason for the formation of the National Commission on Accrediting was to find ways and means of dealing with a large number of accrediting agencies which were having a powerful impact on educational policies." [21] Also he had said, "The primary problem basic to accreditation is the problem of the division of responsibility and authority. We felt that the only possible way to bring some kind of order out of chaos from our point of view was to get the educational institutions united in some kind of stand." [22] With the vast majority of the eligible colleges and universities becoming institutional members within a year, an appearance of unity developed which, however, wavered as soon as the commission began to proclaim policies on major issues in accrediting.[23]

When the National Commission sought support for its attack against the American Chemical Society or the American Association of University Women,[24] or when it asked its members "not to enter into accrediting relationships with agencies not accrediting prior to October 29, 1950," [25] it received support from its constituent members and verbal acclaim from college and university presidents—many of whom, when they were back in their own offices under the many local pressures, continued dealing with these organizations just as before. When the commission directed the accrediting groups to make changes in their policies and procedures some endeavored to comply, while others, the more intrenched and secure, resisted and publicly objected to any attempts at outside dictation over their activities. When the commission enlarged its membership to include junior colleges and teachers

[20] See Note 38, p. 107.   [21] Gustavson   (88).   [22] Brumbaugh   (32). [23] See Note 39, p. 107.   [24] See Note 40, p. 107.   [25] National Commission on Accrediting (142), January 7, 1952.

colleges and when it decided to place major reliance on the regional associations to help solve the excessive problems of professional accrediting, one of its most important constituent members, the Association of American Universities, objected and called a special meeting to review the situation and decide whether it should entirely withdraw its support from the commission.[26]

In reviewing the situation, Harold W. Dodds, then president of the Association of American Universities and president of Princeton University, reported that "we are going toward a condition in which the institutions represented in AAU . . . will have to consider whether they must not 'go it alone' in accrediting, and some other matters as well." Then adding a personal comment he expressed the opinion of the presidents of a group of similarly influential institutions when he stated, "I am not sure that the time has not come when the universities that comprise our Association should begin to think of factoring themselves out of the stream of eighteen hundred colleges and junior colleges and some so-called universities." [27] Despite these opinions the AAU did not officially "factor itself out" of the National Commission; instead it voted to reconsider the question at the end of a period of three years and asked for a report at that time. When that time came the members of AAU were then less interested in criticizing the commission and objecting to accrediting and more concerned about other pressing problems. No further actions were taken.

In describing these early days of the National Commission on Accrediting, one of its most severe critics, Ewald B. Nyquist, Deputy Commissioner of Education for the State of New York, and also for many years Chairman of the Commission on Institutions of Higher Education for the Middle States Association of Colleges and Secondary Schools, has said:

[26] See Note 41, p. 108.   [27] Association of Graduate Schools (10), 1953.

Communications on specific matters from the National Commission after its inception were often confusing, sometimes unrealistic, and not infrequently illustrated the practice of the adoption in advance of arbitrary positions. At any rate, the initial activity of the National Commission touched off a first-class ferment in higher education. . . .

I am sure that the National Commission on Accrediting has certain important accomplishments to its credit: It has stimulated all accrediting agencies to examine their purposes and objectives. It has certainly reduced abuses in accrediting. It has contained accreditation and confined it to certain limits and agencies. It has provided accrediting at large with a definite purpose and objectives which accrediting did not have before. It has, in effect, provided a firm basis for national development of accrediting activity.[28]

OBSERVATIONS

Despite any mistakes which the National Commission may have made in its early years of turmoil it now is witnessing a time of calm and relative good feeling among almost all individuals who are responsible for the accrediting functions of the various national and regional associations. A growing appreciation for the need of wide cooperation has encouraged all regional associations to assume responsibilities for accrediting and to agree to deal only with those professional accrediting agencies recognized by the commission. In turn, the commission has been able to require nearly all the professional agencies to meet certain standards, which include cooperation with each regional association; and it has been able to recognize no more than one agency to a professional field, to encourage all agencies to restudy their policies and practices, and appreciably to limit the number of professional associations entering the field of accrediting.

But these achievements, substantial as they may be, have been attained largely through a negative approach of restraint.

[28] Nyquist (160).

Much more on a positive basis needs to be accomplished, especially in view of the dynamic social changes taking place and the rapidly increasing demands on higher education. Leadership is required—as Frank H. Bowles, president of the College Entrance Examination Board, observed almost a decade ago:

The answer to the problem of mitigating the ills and emphasizing the values of accreditation lies in leadership. And the assumption of leadership in accreditation is a natural charge upon those who have assumed leadership in criticism and objection. They may choose not to exercise this leadership. In such cases their objections and criticisms will become sterile, and this has happened in the past.[29]

It may be added that it happens again and again when the presidents of some of this country's superior colleges and universities consider their institutions to be above accrediting and disdainfully refuse to offer any assistance in finding ways to improve this native method of control of academic standards, an activity which they personally resent and have severely attacked.[30]

The needed leadership in accrediting will be attained only by the method described by David D. Henry when he was president of Wayne University and before he was president of the University of Illinois and president of the National Commission on Accrediting:

The task is complex and will require considerable energy and time on the part of a large number of people and organizations. Its completion will require educational statesmanship, and a willingness on the part of all working with the problems to place educational goals and services to the public above all other considerations.[31]

This statement confronts the colleges and universities of the country with a vital question. Is there sufficient enlighten-

[29] Bowles (25).   [30] See Note 42, p. 108.   [31] Henry (100).

ment and determination among educators and organizations to provide the consistent statesmanship presently needed for the improvement of accreditation—our native method of controlling academic standards?

EIGHT

Enlightenment

THE HISTORY of accreditation can be written much more easily than its future can be foretold. Whether in art, athletics, politics, science, or education, there always is a risk in any attempt to make predictions. Yet with increasing demands being placed upon higher education and with accreditation growing in importance, the future of this native phenomenon should be considered and not left entirely to chance.

We have learned that accrediting was developed and fashioned as a result of well defined historical forces. From this fact we may confidently assume that its future course will likewise be shaped by forces which are exerting themselves on society today. These forces, which are numerous and widespread, need to be reviewed in relation to their implications for accrediting.

WORLD WIDE FORCES

Many contemporary factors are affecting the destiny of the world's population more extensively and more rapidly than any previous combination of forces in the entire history of mankind. Long held doctrines and beliefs are being subjected to review and possible annihilation, while, under the threat of disaster, new and dynamic issues are pleading for resolution. Not even our social and political structures are immune from attack. Doubts are continually being raised as to their adequacy in meeting the demands of the future.

In fact all mankind is facing a series of revolutions whose magnitude cannot be calculated adequately at this time. Bursting populations, scientific discoveries, technological developments, and rapid communication are forcing economic, political, and social realignments for all peoples and also are supporting the foundations of new ideologies. Throughout the world broad social changes are taking place as the majority of the population of the globe rebel against conditions of undernourishment, low living standards, and racial barriers under which they and their forbears have existed for centuries. Suddenly millions are being released from colonial rule at a period in history when the sinister aspects of atomic energy are exerting an influence on international political alignments in a manner similar to, but more profound than, the influence of gunpowder on the early development of the modern state. While these transformations are taking place, the population of the world, increasing at a rate sufficient to double itself in half a century, is spreading over all possible productive land. Space, which in previous generations served as an outlet for social tensions, can be expected in the future only to increase stress and strain.

Land space, however, is not the only element which will be inadequate for the future. Other natural resources will be deficient for the rising standard of living demanded by all peoples, and not merely by the peoples of the Atlantic nations whose 16 per cent of the world population presently consumes 70 per cent of the world's income.[1] Of all nations, none has ever been more wealthy nor more profligate than the United States, whose consumption of metals and mineral fuels in the past forty years alone has exceeded the total consumed by the whole of mankind in all preceding history.[2] With the means now developed for rapid transmission of knowledge and ideas, one may confidently anticipate an increasingly insistent demand on the part of the non-white majority of the global population not merely for a rising standard of living but for what they will consider to be a more equable share of the natural resources of the world. What is more, these demands will have their impact on the social and political structure of this country.

NATIONAL FORCES

Equalling these external influences are forces within the United States which also are causing profound readjustments. A spirit of laissez-faire with maximum decentralization of government was suitable for a rural, sparsely populated, expansive and isolated country with slow communication and apparently unlimited natural resources—but not for a mobile, urban, extremely interdependent population with a high standard of living and decreasing natural resources. To meet these rapidly changing conditions, the extent and responsibilities of the federal government have been greatly enlarged in almost a single generation. Recognition of the need to protect and enhance the welfare of the people has been shown by the relatively recent actions of the national government to regulate the economy, support prices for agriculture, prohibit child labor, develop hydro-electric power, provide

[1] Ward (216).   [2] Huxley (113).

job and social security, guarantee bank deposits, regulate securities exchanges, provide for slum clearance, and support the right of workingmen to organize.

These activities, formerly condemned as incompatible with virtuous American traditions, are now taken for granted by a large proportion of the population of the country at the same time as additional social needs are pressing for further government planning and intervention. It is widely recognized now that only government can provide the means to solve the already present and complex problems of mass transportation, municipal and area rehabilitation, and conservation of depleted natural resources—and that only government can provide most of the funds required to construct high energy accelerators and nuclear reactors, conduct research on atomic power, and develop methods of controlling weather. What is more, conditions may soon develop in such a way that only government will be capable of providing sufficient facilities for the education of most of the trained and educated citizens whom the growing and increasingly interdependent population is requiring in larger and larger numbers.

Despite temporary setbacks federal and state governments together will undoubtedly provide in the future most of the facilities needed for higher education which now is the only gateway for entrance to most professions and which has become necessary for advancement in many vocations. No political party will long fail to heed the public clamor for educational opportunities for its children, nor long fail to recognize that higher education in the United States is becoming a matter of national concern—for survival.

INFLUENCES ON HIGHER EDUCATION

These forces, both world wide and national, are creating the need for increasingly larger units for planning, organization, and control and are adding to the multiplying com-

plexities of modern life. Changes are taking place in society
with such breathtaking speed that enlightenment and imagination of the highest order are needed to cope with the new
situations. This need applies no less to education than to
business, labor, government, or the military. Yet the leaders
in higher education continue to be so preoccupied with their
individual responsibilities that they find it difficult to contem-
plate the future of education on a national basis.

Historically education in the United States has been a local
responsibility. Founded to meet almost every community am-
bition or sectarian desire, colleges and universities have shared
intimately in the American heritage of laissez-faire and intense competition. Presidents of colleges and universities,
nurtured in this tradition and faced with the onerous com-
mitment of locating sufficient finances to keep their institutions
alive and independent, have found it difficult to think of
education from other than a local point of view. Alumni, on
whose loyalty the future existence of most private colleges
depends, lend their support to the memory of bygone years.
Likewise most faculty members, educated through the path
of independent research, develop an image of education that
frequently is limited to the range of their own specialties.
It is not surprising that educational institutions, in the words
of David Riesman, "are among the last strongholds of the free
enterprise system." [3]

At the very time when education itself is struggling to
adjust to social changes that may eventually affect its very
foundations, all humanity is relying on education for guidance
and direction, as well as new knowledge. Fabulous discoveries,
whether in archaeology or in science, in diggings of the past
or in flights to outer space, are opening the eyes of man to
a panorama of the world and the universe for which his
vision is not yet in focus. These discoveries, which are under-

[3] Riesman (189).

mining doctrines and dogmas formerly considered incontrovertible, are being revealed in the libraries and laboratories of many universities through the stimulus of man's insatiable curiosity and the competition of governments for national survival. These same discoveries are requiring educators to deal with new ideas and methods, and to encounter problems more grave than any that have ever previously faced the colleges and universities of this country.

Despite protests stemming from tradition, local pride and sectarian independence, higher education is being forced to conceive of itself in a larger framework. Not merely government but all segments of society—business, labor, finance, farmers, the military, and the public—are placing increasing reliance on institutions of higher learning. Faced with the necessity of providing educational opportunities for hundreds of thousands of new students, of supporting research on an ever widening horizon, of attracting trained personnel, and of locating adequate financing for these activities in a period of steady inflation, the presidents and other leaders in higher education are finding themselves engulfed in the complexities of modern life. Having been raised in the tradition of educational free enterprise, these educators may be excused if they seem bewildered by the transformation of their institutions within a generation from places of unhurried study and reverie, seldom disturbed by more than youthful pranks, to bustling centers of multitudinous activities, all affecting not only the students and faculties but some phase of the national welfare. Committed to the heritage of freedom to explore, to inquire, to investigate—a freedom fundamental to Western civilization—educators are confronted with the dilemma of maintaining this cardinal principle as education, like all modern society, becomes more organized and structured than in the past.

In facing this very same dilemma the authors of the recent

report, *Pursuit of Excellence: Manpower and Education*, offered only one solution:

The notion that we might escape the complexities of modern life by returning to some simpler form of existence is sheer romancing. The interlocking complexities of modern society are an inescapable part of our future: if we are to nourish individual freedom we shall have to nourish it under these circumstances. If we are to maintain individual creativity we shall have to learn to preserve it in a context of organization . . .[4]

In the same way it is sheer romancing to hope for the day when there will be no accreditation and to assume that individual creativity cannot flourish as long as accrediting exists. In modern society, higher education can function adequately only with the aid of some organizational method that maintains academic standards. However, for the sake of both education and society, these standards must be established and enforced with enlightenment and imagination.

INFLUENCES ON ACCREDITATION

Leaders in higher education who have been bewildered by transformations in colleges and universities have been even more perplexed by the growing importance of accreditation. It has been difficult for them to realize that increasing reliance on lists of approved institutions is a natural corollary both to a more structured society and to an expanding interest in higher education on the part of all segments of society. Professional people seek to insure their livelihood by protecting themselves from inadequately trained competitors. Prospective students, whether native or foreign, wish assurance of quality in colleges and universities. Government officials and corporation officers require confirmation of at least the minimum competence of institutions, while the public and the institutions themselves need protection from fraud and

[4] Rockfeller Brothers Fund (190), p. 14.

deception. As society places greater dependence on lists of accredited institutions, the accrediting agencies themselves share an increasing responsibility to maintain an influence that is constructive and stimulating and not constricting and stultifying. Unfortunately this has not always been the case.

As we have seen, excessive demands and narrow requirements of many professional agencies caused opposition to their former activities and gave support to the creation of the Joint Committee on Accrediting in 1938 and subsequently to the formation of the National Commission on Accrediting in 1949. Detailed, specific, factual, and outdated criteria encouraged dissatisfaction and led to the North Central Association's study of the early 1930's which forced a major revision in accrediting on the part of most agencies. Studies of the ineffectiveness of accreditation as conducted by the Association of American Universities helped to cause that organization in 1948 to abandon its practice of accrediting and, most unfortunately, to disregard its responsibility of helping to maintain academic standards in the other institutions of higher learning in the country. Today there is further uneasiness and uncertainty as many educators ask: Is accrediting serving as a sufficient stimulus to colleges and universities which must adjust rapidly to world wide and national forces?

In the ebb and flow of history there is always, on the one hand, a desire for stability and consolidation and, on the other, an urge for revision and reconstruction. Sometimes the current flows one way, and sometimes the other. For the present there is no doubt that stimulation for revision and reconstruction is in greater need than protection for the status quo which some accrediting agencies are accused of fostering.

During recent years professional accrediting agencies have been required to justify their policies and requirements not only to their professions but to the institutions which are subject to accreditation. On various occasions presidents and other university officials have threatened agencies representing professional interests with demise if they did not improve their accrediting policies. In contrast, regional associations, which like trade associations are organized for service to their members and for self-enforcement of standards, have been required to justify their policies and requirements to no one except their own membership. An obligation to the public does exist by implication, but enforcement rests completely on the will of the institutional members. Recognizing the potential danger in this situation, Manning M. Pattillo, Associate Director of the Lilly Endowment and formerly Associate Secretary of the Commission on Colleges and Universities of the North Central Association, wrote when he was in his former position:

If the delicate balance between the institutional and the public interest in general accrediting is disturbed so that the scales become heavily weighted on the institutional side, we shall see other instrumentalities developed to serve the public interest in accrediting.[5]

A possible foretaste of this eventuality may be seen in the formation during the past decade of three regional boards—the Southern Regional Education Board, the Western Interstate Commission for Higher Education, and the New England Board of Higher Education—each created for the study, development, and coordination of higher education in its respective geographical area. With official backing from the governors and state legislatures, these boards have developed and are operating various cooperative arrangements among colleges and universities in all the states of these three sections of the country. Their policies are based on the principle that economy and effectiveness in higher education can be obtained best through cooperation among the educational institutions of a region. Supported by most of the large

[5] Pattillo (162).

universities, these recent organizations are providing a stimulation to higher education, including professional education, which the regional accrediting associations at least a quarter of a century earlier were urged to provide. Because the regional associations failed to heed this advice, "other instrumentalities developed to serve the public interest" as Pattillo predicted might happen in the case of accrediting.[6]

Consequently, one may logically pose the question, as a few educators already are doing: Will other agencies, and especially governmental agencies, be developed to serve the public interest in accrediting?

VOLUNTARY OR GOVERNMENTAL ACCREDITATION?

For many years suggestions have been made that "the time may eventually arrive when the functions of accrediting educational institutions can be taken over entirely by some governmental agency, thus changing the process from an extra-legal to a legal control." [7] Every proposal of this type has been greeted with dozens of refutations based on the political traditions of this country. An ardent advocate of these political traditions, Harold W. Dodds, then president of Princeton University, implied his opposition to governmental control of academic standards when he included the following statement in a speech entitled "Relation of the Federal Government to Higher Education."

A democratic state, as contrasted with a totalitarian, must cultivate within itself voluntary and non-political organs of opinion. It cannot rely upon public officers or political parties to originate and present policies of public welfare. Lord Acton's assertion that "liberty is possible only in a society where there are centers of organization other than political" has been amply sustained in recent years. One grave danger to democracy is the tendency for voluntary societies to abdicate in favor of a government in which paid people do the work . . .[8]

[6] See Note 43, p. 109.   [7] Russell and Judd (193), p. 159.   [8] Dodds (69).

One very grave danger to the future of accrediting by voluntary accrediting associations is the fact that they have lost the interest of most of the presidents of the outstanding colleges and universities throughout the country and are suffering from a lack of this type of leadership and support.

The accrediting associations are on trial as they have never been before. On occasions in the past they encountered criticism, overcame opposition, and continued to exert a powerful influence on higher education. Today the rush of events is so swift, the pressure of world wide and national forces so pervasive, and the magnitude of the problems confronting the institutions of higher learning so boundless, that society is calling for imagination and enlightened initiative in the establishment and enforcement of academic standards for the colleges and universities.

Can the accrediting associations respond to this call? The answer depends upon the leadership in higher education. Just as the fate of democracy rests upon an informed electorate and responsible leadership, so the future of accreditation with its struggle over standards in higher education depends upon educational leaders who are enlightened, who consider education from a national—even a global—point of view, and who will recognize and assume their educational responsibilities.

Epilogue

PRESIDENT EDWARD TYLER's letter of irritation was never written to that "impertinent accrediting agency." His initial annoyance was overcome by curiosity, and curiosity led him to study and finally understand accreditation to be a means of controlling and improving academic standards.

Tyler's understanding, however, in no way abated his sense of unhappiness, even disagreement, with the written report sent to Enfield University by that professional accrediting association. On the other hand, his search for information did teach him that accrediting is a fallible method of evaluating and judging institutions or programs of study, that it uses only broad and gross measurements, and that this system is consistent with the heritage and traditions of this country.

Convinced from his short experience that to maintain and

to improve college and university standards in the United States some form of accreditation is necessary, and convinced that this activity again is in need of revisions to meet changing conditions, Tyler decided that improvements would not be instituted merely as a result of complaints and criticisms. He must actively share in the responsibility of reviewing and revising accrediting policies and procedures and of fostering a spirit for improving other institutions as well as his own. Additionally, since both the social and the educational implications of accreditation are broad and diverse, and since its problems are intricate and involved, he must concentrate his attention on a few issues which seem to him to be the most important at this time, such as:

> *What criteria in accrediting can be developed which place relatively less emphasis on minimum standards and more on continued institutional re-evaluation, experimentation and improvement?*

> *How can accrediting be made more stimulating for institutions of quality?*

> *How can the inevitable increase in the accreditation of graduate schools be designed without impairment of independent research and individual scholarship?*

> *How can the needs for assurance of quality in specialized institutions and in additional professional programs of study be met without increasing the number of separate professional accrediting agencies?*

> *How can accrediting be simplified without limiting its effectiveness?*

> *How can accrediting adequately satisfy the needs of various groups and of the public for more in-*

formation about the degree of quality of individual institutions?

How can the growing interests in higher education on the part of government be met without increasing its involvement in accreditation?

As President Tyler reflected on these and other problems confronting higher education he was reminded of a comment in the *Second Report to the President* from the President's Committee on Education Beyond the High School. He knew of no statement that more aptly expressed his conviction about accrediting—"Either Federal standardization or local apathy would be fatal to the best interests of education." [1]

[1] President's Committee on Education (173), p. 106.

Notes

1. At the present time the National Commission on Accrediting recognizes twenty-two professional accrediting agencies and the United States Commissioner of Education recognizes twenty-five.
2. Each year on an average, 10 per cent of the colleges and universities listed by the United States Office of Education *(Educational Directory, Part 3: Higher Education)* appoint a new president. This information was derived from statistics furnished by Theresa B. Wilkins, Research Assistant, United States Office of Education.
3. As a consequence of influences from the United States following the Second World War, accrediting has been introduced as a partial means of control of academic standards for the universities in both the Philippines and Japan. Some observers have questioned the wisdom

and effectiveness of attempting to transplant this peculiarly singular educational activity to countries with traditions and heritage totally different from the United States.

4. The definition of accrediting employed by G. F. Zook and M. E. Haggerty in *The Evaluation of Higher Institutions*, Vol. I: *Principles of Accrediting Higher Institutions* (Chicago: University of Chicago Press, 1936), p. 18 is: "Accreditment is the recognition accorded to an educational institution in the United States by means of inclusion in a list of institutions issued by some agency or organization which sets up standards or requirements that must be complied with in order to secure approval."

5. Although "there is in Canada no official accrediting agency, the National Conference of Canadian Universities might be described as fulfilling the functions of such an agency . . . Membership within N.C.C.U. is generally accepted by an accrediting agency within the U.S.A. as being an adequate indication that the institution is of university standing . . . Since 1957 the N.C.C.U. has been charged with the distribution of federal grants to all universities and colleges in Canada." —Excerpts from letter, dated February 13, 1959, to author from J. Rosemary Bushnell, Research Assistant, National Conference of Canadian Universities, Ottawa, Canada.

6. In 1908 the Commonwealth of Kentucky was upheld on the basis of employing part of its reserved power in its attempt to amend or repeal the charter of Berea College. Berea College v. Commonwealth of Kentucky, 211 U.S. 45, 53 L. Ed. 81, 29 S. Ct. 33, (1908), affirming Ky. 209, 94 S.W. 623, (1906).

"The Berea College case of 1908 demonstrated that

although reservations may be properly made for purposes of amending, altering, or repealing corporate charters, such reservations must be applied reasonably and consistently."—Clark Spurlock, *Education and the Supreme Court* (Urbana: University of Illinois Press, 1955), p. 28.

7. Between 1840 and 1888 school attendance increased 520 per cent. Mortimer J. Adler and Milton Mayer, *The Revolution in Education* (Chicago: University of Chicago Press, 1958), p. 9.

8. At least 75 per cent of the students in the West and in the South must have been prepared for college by the colleges themselves in their own preparatory departments. John Eaton, *Annual Report of the Commissioner*, United States Bureau of Education, 1873, p. XLVIII.

9. "By 1897 there were 42 state colleges and about 150 other institutions in which some form of certifying system of admission was in use."—Edwin S. Broome, *A Historical and Critical Discussion of College Admission Requirements* (New York: The Macmillan Co., 1903), p. 118.

10. After many years of deliberation the Southern Association of Colleges and Secondary Schools voted at its annual meeting in 1956 to accept into full membership qualified colleges for Negro youth.

11. (a) An organization with the title Western Association of Colleges and Secondary Schools had a tenuous existence from 1931 to March 1, 1950 when it disbanded after the Western College Association decided to become an active regional accrediting association. Information obtained from a personal letter, dated December 16, 1958, to the author from Charles T. Fitts, former secretary of the Western College Association.

(b) The territories included in each of the regional

associations are listed as follows: *Middle States Association:* Canal Zone, Delaware, District of Columbia, Maryland, New Jersey, New York, Pennsylvania and Puerto Rico. *New England Association:* Connecticut, Maine, Massachusetts, New Hampshire, Rhode Island and Vermont. *North Central Association:* Arizona, Arkansas, Colorado, Illinois, Indiana, Iowa, Kansas, Michigan, Minnesota, Missouri, Nebraska, New Mexico, North Dakota, Ohio, Oklahoma, South Dakota, West Virginia, Wisconsin and Wyoming. *Northwest Association:* Alaska, Hawaii (secondary schools), Idaho, Montana, Nevada, Oregon, Utah and Washington. *Southern Association:* Alabama, Florida, Georgia, Kentucky, Louisiana, Mississippi, North Carolina, South Carolina, Tennessee, Texas and Virginia. *Western College Association:* California, Guam and Hawaii (higher institutions).

12. In contrast to the policy developed by the Middle States Association whereby a large team of visitors, including representatives of professional accrediting agencies, simultaneously visit an institution on a ten year cycle, the North Central Association devised a much more simple procedure. Since the latter association, which includes the immense territory of nineteen states, required revisits to an accredited institution only when there was apparent cause for investigation, the policy was adopted of appointing a "generalist" to accompany the team of inspectors from a professional agency whenever the president of the university so requested. The generalist is usually a member of the central administration of a comparable university. In addition to this program, the North Central Association is now embarking on a modest and exploratory schedule of regular revisits to accredited institutions.

13. On February 27, 1959 Foster Furcolo, Governor of the Commonwealth of Massachusetts, addressed a letter to President Dwight D. Eisenhower calling to his attention the fact that some regional accrediting associations employ a specific teacher-student ratio as one of the criteria for the accreditation of colleges and universities. This letter forcefully points out that to date few, if any studies have proven the validity of this requirement and that the situation requires careful study. The governor also proposed that if it should prove necessary the study should be conducted by a special presidentially appointed commission. Letter from Governor Furcolo printed in the United States *Congressional Record* on March 18, 1959.

14. This same policy did not apply to every agency of the federal government. For over fifty years the United States Department of Agriculture has exercised the responsibility of visiting and accrediting colleges of veterinary medicine in connection with the employment of veterinarians under Civil Service regulations. As a result of suggestions initiated in 1957 by the National Commission on Accrediting, this practice is being reviewed by the Agricultural Research Services of the Department of Agriculture with the intention of relying on the American Veterinary Medical Association, a recognized accrediting agency, for the lists of qualified schools.

    In contrast to the Department of Agriculture's long practice, the Veterans' Administration and the United States Public Health Service, when they needed lists of approved graduate programs in counseling and clinical psychology at the end of the Second World War, requested the American Psychological Association to provide such lists in place of undertaking the evaluations themselves.

15. Such government divisions as the Civil Service Commission, Selective Service, the Veterans' Administration, the Department of Defense, the Department of State, and the Department of Health, Education and Welfare place almost complete dependence on this publication, as well as on the annual *Educational Directory, Part 3: Higher Education,* for which there is a slightly broader basis for inclusion.

16. The University of the State of New York was organized in such a way that it could grant the degrees on authorization of the Board of Regents to those who completed their courses of study at newly established colleges. This projected pattern of control as intended by Alexander Hamilton never materialized. Andrew D. White, first president of Cornell University, and others renewed the proposal, but nothing came of this encouragement.

17. "More than 200 such colleges and universities were discovered, with operating addresses in at least 37 states." —Robert H. Reid, *American Degree Mills.* (Washington: American Council on Education, January 20, 1959), p. 4. Draft of study in process of publication.

"A distinction should be made between fraudulent schools of the type described and legitimate home study schools which conduct courses through correspondence. The latter schools which were first established in the 1890's number today over 450 and enroll probably as many as 750,000 individuals taking mostly vocational courses. Because of inadequate legal control these legitimate home study schools organized the National Home Study Council in 1926 to protect their own interests against fraudulence and the Council recently has developed its own accrediting program for its member schools."—H. Allion and H. Kempfer, *Private Home Study in the United States* (Washington: National Home Study Council, 1956).

18. On April 7, 1958 the Governor of California approved a bill passed by the State Legislature which made material changes in the law relating to the issuance of degrees and diplomas by private institutions. Assembly Bill No. 6, Chapter 13, Statutes of 1958, First Extraordinary Session. (A.B. 6).

19. No record of this resolution could be found in the official minutes in the office of the National Council of Chief State School Officers although the resolution is quoted in the report prepared by Fred J. Kelly, *et al.*, *College Accreditation by Agencies Within States*, United States Office of Education Bulletin 1940, No. 3.

20. Letter to author from Eugene B. Elliott, December 5, 1958, former chief state school officer in the State of Michigan and former officer of the National Council of Chief State School Officers.

21. There are over 600 institutions outside the State of New York which have curriculums registered with the Board of Regents.

22. Professions in which licensure requirements give strong support to accrediting include: architecture, dentistry, engineering, medicine, nursing, optometry, osteopathy, pharmacy, poditary, and veterinary medicine. In law, in which there is accrediting, it is not called licensure but admission to the bar. Other professions in which there is accrediting and in which legislation requiring licensure has been enacted only in recent years in a few states are forestry, landscape architecture, psychology, and social work. There is no licensure, for example, in chemistry and journalism, in which there is accrediting.

23. An example of the respect for the accomplishments of the medical profession is shown by the following quotation from a paper read by a former Yale law school professor before the Section of Legal Education and Admissions to the Bar of the American Bar Association on September 4, 1917: "Surely it is not too much to hope that the time has now come when we of the legal profession will refuse longer to lag so far behind our brethren of the medical profession in our standards of education and of admission to the practice of our honorable profession."—Walter W. Cook, "Improvement of Legal Education and of Standards for Admission to the Bar," *American Law School Review*, 4 (December 1917), pp. 338-45.

24. The Association of American Law Schools, which was organized in 1900 through the encouragement of the American Bar Association, employs standards and procedures for membership of schools which classify it as an accrediting agency, despite protests to the contrary from some of its members. The standards are somewhat more severe than those employed by the American Bar Association. Slightly over 80 per cent of the ABA accredited law schools have been admitted to membership in the Association of American Law Schools.

25. Some individuals believe that the professional accrediting agencies should take a more aggressive role, as evidenced by the following quotation: "The Bench and Bar of America can *force* [italics mine] if only they would, the colleges and universities of America to do an about-face."—John G. Hervey, "The Decline of Professionalism in the Law: An Exploration into Some Causes," *New York Law Forum*, 3, No. 4 (October 1957).

26. Additional national professional agencies maintain accrediting activities for the following fields of study: archi-

tecture, design, journalism, nurse anesthesiology, osteopathy, podiatry, public health, and religious education. Following the Second World War accrediting was also inaugurated for bible schools and colleges as well as noncollegiate schools of business, in both cases primarily so that these schools would be eligible for the enrollment of veterans under the G.I. Bill of Rights.

27. These are architecture, dentistry, engineering, forestry, journalism, law, library science, medicine, music, nursing, social work, and teacher education. In addition, grants have been made to the Middle States and the North Central accrediting associations.

28. In each of the professions, with the exception of teacher education, accrediting developed before licensure. In the case of teacher education just the opposite situation has prevailed. Certification of teachers for the public schools, at first locally and then by the states, preceded the accreditation of programs of study in teacher education.

29. "Past experience indicates that accreditation by professional associations tends to be more exacting than accreditation by associations of schools giving professional training. The practitioners are adversely affected by poorly trained professionals . . ."—Myron Lieberman, *Education as a Profession* (Englewood Cliffs, New Jersey: Prentice-Hall, Inc., 1956), p. 164.

30. A study in 1919 revealed that twenty-two of the 72 universities studied allowed faculties no choice in decisions on questions of educational policy. George G. Bogert, "Historical Survey of Faculty Participation in University Government in the United States," John Dale Russell and Donald M. Mackenzie, eds., *Emergent Responsibilities in Higher Education* (Chicago: University of Chicago Press, 1946).

31. The American Association of University Professors created a Committee on Accreditation in 1957 solely for the purpose of serving as a means of keeping its membership better informed on developments in accrediting and of encouraging the use of faculty members on visiting teams of the regional accrediting associations.

32. Between 1940 and 1952 the proportion of college students majoring in liberal arts and sciences dropped from 43 per cent to 35.7 per cent. Mortimer J. Adler and Milton Mayer, *The Revolution in Education* (Chicago: University of Chicago Press, 1958), p. 91.

33. As of December 1955, over 60 per cent of the then 1,247 regionally accredited institutions offered no programs of study which were accredited by a professional agency. Less than 20 per cent offered only one professionally accredited program, whereas about 20 per cent of the regionally accredited institutions offered two or more professionally accredited programs which in turn represented 85 per cent of the professionally accredited programs offered by the regionally accredited institutions.

34. The committees appointed by the American Council on Education to consider matters relating to accrediting are as follows: Committee on College Standards, 1920–1927; Committee on Standards, 1931–1936; Committee on the Study of Accrediting Procedures, 1940–1942; Committee on Accrediting Procedures, 1943–1945; and Committee on Accrediting Procedures in Higher Institutions, 1946 and 1948–1950.

    Almost annually from 1920 to 1935 the American Council on Education published in the *Educational Record* a list of accredited higher institutions. This practice was discontinued in 1936 when the Executive

Committee recognized that many individuals were incorrectly assuming that the council was an accrediting agency. *Educational Record,* 17 (July 1936), p. 514.

35. A study in 1940 showed that thirty-three accrediting agencies included 2,611 items on their questionnaires of which 61 per cent were similar and only thirty-nine per cent were different. Lawrence L. Bethel, "The Historical Development and Present Status of Procedures for Accreditation of American Colleges and Universities," doctoral dissertation, Yale University, 1940. Mimeographed.

36. In 1948 when the Association of American Universities discontinued its accrediting, there were 339 institutions on its approved list, or 19.6 per cent of those listed by the United States Office of Education. At this time the regional associations had accredited 923 institutions, 53.3 per cent of the Office of Education list. B. E. Blanchard, "Accredited Higher Institutions During 1948," *Journal of Educational Research,* 44 (January 1951), pp. 353-62.

37. The number of foreign nationals enrolled in colleges and universities in the United States has increased markedly in only a few years. During the year 1958–1959 the total is nearly 50,000, a number much larger than the total number of students enrolled in such institutions in many other countries.

Donald J. Shank, Executive Vice-President of the Institute of International Education, in a letter to the author dated October 2, 1958, has stated: ". . . the list of AAU approved schools . . . had begun to be accepted as one measure of quality by a number of foreign institutions and foreign governments . . . It did have the advantage of providing one relatively simple list of good undergraduate colleges. The fact that the names of many of the member institutions of the AAU were known overseas also gave the list a certain prestige which has not been transferred to the several regional accrediting associations."

In order that degrees awarded in this country may currently receive adequate recognition in many other countries, the United States Office of Education is frequently requested to attach a certifying statement indicating the validity of the degree.

38. The original constituent membership of the National Commission on Accrediting comprised the following organizations: American Association of Land-Grant Colleges and State Universities, Association of American Colleges, Association of American Universities, Association of Urban Universities, and National Association of State Universities. In 1951 the American Association of Junior Colleges and the Association of Teacher Education Institutions, the latter especially organized in order that teachers colleges could be represented in the commission, were added as constituent members.

39. By November 1950 there were 640 institutional members; the number was increased later when the junior colleges and the teachers colleges became eligible for membership. The total of the membership now is over eleven hundred colleges and universities, probably the largest institutional membership of any educational organization.

40. Even though the American Association of University Women insisted that its college approval program was not accrediting, it boasted at the same time that it "has been a pioneer in establishing and maintaining standards in institutions of higher learning."—J. C. Moncure, "Accrediting Conference of the American Council on Edu-

cation," *Journal of the American Association of University Women*, 32 (June 1939), pp. 240–242.

There are presently 423 colleges and universities on the approved list of AAUW. *Journal of the American Association of University Women*, 52 (March 1959), p. 186.

41. At the time the Association of American Universities was questioning the policies of the National Commission on Accrediting and debating whether to continue its support, the presidents of ten of the then thirty-seven AAU member universities were serving among the forty-two Commissioners of the National Commission on Accrediting. It may also be noted that the Association of American Universities has the smallest membership of any of the seven constituent members of the National Commission.

42. It is interesting to note that one of the few points which the presidents of some of the most influential universities have in common with the presidents of many of the non-regionally accredited colleges is a sense of frustration and unhappiness with accrediting—but primarily for different reasons.

In 1956 the presidents of approximately half the non-regionally accredited, non-tax supported, liberal arts colleges organized the Council for Advancement of Small Colleges in a collective attempt to present their financial needs to the public and to improve their educational status so that individually they might gain accreditation. At that time 295 was the median enrollment of the fifty-two institutions in the council and their dates of founding extended as far back as the 1840's. A. T. Hill, "What is a Non-accredited College?" in *Educational Record*, 38 (October 1957), pp. 348–354.

Of all the non-regionally accredited higher institutions included in the *Educational Directory, Part 3: Higher Education for the year 1954–55*, 23.05 per cent were bachelor-degree granting institutions, 30.53 per cent were junior colleges, and 46.42 per cent offered special programs of study. Of the bachelor-degree granting institutions: 19.59 per cent were tax-supported, 31.76 per cent were related to a Protestant denomination, 23.65 per cent were affiliated with the Roman Catholic Church, and 25 per cent were independent; 60.13 per cent had enrollments of less than 300 while only 22.3 per cent had enrollments over 500.

43. Over the years various cooperative arrangements among different colleges and universities have been developed of which few appear to have been either initiated or suggested by regional accrediting associations. Within recent months, completely independently of any regional association, ten medium sized independent colleges formed an organization, the Associated Colleges of the Midwest, for the purpose of conducting cooperative studies and exploring ways of providing improved and more efficient education. In addition, eleven large midwest, private and tax-supported universities are now collectively studying methods whereby unnecessary duplication may be reduced and cooperation increased.

Bibliography

THIS SELECTIVE bibliography of books, articles and speeches on the subject of accreditation has been compiled to assist those wishing to pursue further study of this educational activity. Supplementing the items which relate directly to accrediting, a few additional references have been included for those who may wish to study accrediting in relation to other educational and social developments. Attention is also directed to the volume, *Accreditation in Higher Education*, recently edited by Lloyd E. Blauch, which contains at the end of each chapter a list of references.

1. ABBOTT, FRANK C., Ed. *Faculty-Administration Relationships*. Washington: American Council on Education, 1958.
2. ABBOTT, FRANK C. *Government Policy and Higher Education: A Study of the Regents of the University*

of the State of New York: 1784–1949. New York: Cornell University Press, 1958.

3. ADLER, MORTIMER J., and MAYER, MILTON. *The Revolution in Education*. Chicago: University of Chicago Press, 1958.

4. ALLEN, RAYMOND B. *Medical Education and the Changing Order*. New York: Commonwealth Fund, 1946.

5. ALLION, H., and KEMPFER, H. *Private Home Study in the U. S.: A Statistical Study*. Washington: National Home Study Council, 1956.

6. AMERICAN COUNCIL ON EDUCATION. *Standards for Accrediting Colleges, Junior Colleges and Teacher Training Institutions*. Washington: the Council, 1924.

7. ARMSBY, H. H. "Accreditation of Engineering Curricula," *Higher Education*, 12 (October 1955), pp. 23–30.

8. ARMSTRONG, W. E. "Developments in the Accreditation of Teacher Education," *National Education Association Journal*, 46 (February 1957), p. 113.

9. ASSOCIATION OF AMERICAN UNIVERSITIES. *Proceedings*. Published annually 1901–1948.

10. ASSOCIATION OF GRADUATE SCHOOLS IN THE ASSOCIATION OF AMERICAN UNIVERSITIES. *Proceedings*. Published annually since 1949.

11. BABCOCK, K .C. "Further Coordination of Colleges and Universities," *Association of American Universities Proceedings*, 1913, pp. 48–55.

12. BABCOCK, K. C. "The Naming of an Approved List of Colleges," *North Central Association of Colleges and Secondary Schools Proceedings*, 1913, pp. 82–103.

13. BABCOCK, K. C. "Present Standards of Voluntary Associations," *Educational Record*, 2 (July 1921), pp. 92–99.

14. BABCOCK, K. C. "Some Needed Revisions in Medical Licensure," *Educational Record*, 4 (April 1923), pp. 59–63.

15. BAKER, CARLOS. *A Friend in Power*. New York: Charles Scribner's Sons, 1958.

16. BEARD, CHARLES A. and MARY A. *The Rise of American Civilization*. New York: The Macmillan Co., 1927.

17. BETHEL, LAWRENCE L. "The Historical Development and Present Status of Procedures for Accreditation of American Colleges and Universities." Ph.D. dissertation, Yale University, 1940.

18. BLACKMAR, FRANK W. *The History of Federal and State Aid to Higher Education*. Washington: Government Printing Office, 1890.

19. BLANCHARD, B. E. "Accredited Higher Institutions During 1948," *Journal of Education Research*, 44 (January 1951), pp. 353–362.

20. BLAUCH, LLOYD E., Ed. *Accreditation in Higher Education*. Washington: U. S. Department of Health, Education, and Welfare, 1959.

21. BLAUCH, LLOYD E., Ed. *Education for the Professions*. Washington: U. S. Department of Health, Education, and Welfare, 1955.

22. BOURNE, RANDOLPH S. "Democracy and University Administration," *Educational Review*, 49 (May 1915), pp. 455–459.

23. BOWLES, FRANK H. "Causes and Effects in Accreditation," *Southern University Conference Proceedings*, 1954, pp. 20–32.

24. BOWLES, FRANK H. "Evaluation of Higher Institutions," *Educational Outlook*, 23 (April 1949), pp. 158–164.

25. BOWLES, FRANK H. "Higher Education Evaluates Accreditation," *Middle States Association of Colleges and Secondary Schools Proceedings*, 1950, pp. 35–39.

26. BOWLES, FRANK H. "Place of the Regional Association in the Future Educational Scene," *Middle States Association of Colleges and Secondary Schools Proceedings*, 1957, pp. 24–36.

27. BRADBY, EDWARD, Ed. *The University Outside Europe.* London: Oxford University Press, 1939.

28. BRODY, ALEXANDER. *The American State and Higher Education.* Washington: American Council on Education, 1935.

29. BRONSON, W. C. *The History of Brown University, 1764–1914.* Providence: Brown University, 1914.

30. BROOME, EDWIN C. *A Historical and Critical Discussion of College Admission Requirements.* New York: The Macmillan Co., 1903.

31. BRUBACHER, JOHN S., and RUDY, WILLIS. *Higher Education in Transition—A History of American Colleges and Universities, 1636–1956.* New York: Harper & Brothers, 1958.

32. BRUMBAUGH, A. J. "The Accrediting Agencies Face Their Common Problems," *Educational Record*, 31 (January 1950), pp. 59–92.

33. BRYCE, JAMES. *The American Commonwealth* (2 vols.). New York: The Macmillan Co., 1917.

34. BURNS, NORMAN. "Some Thoughts on the Theory and Practice of Accrediting," *North Central Association Quarterly*, 28 (October 1953), pp. 205–214.

35. BUTLER, NICHOLAS MURRAY. *Across the Busy Years.* New York: Charles Scribner's Sons, 1939.

36. CALIFORNIA, ASSEMBLY OF THE STATE OF; ASSEMBLY INTERIM COMMITTEE ON EDUCATION. *Progress Report of Sub-Committee on Issuance of Degrees, 1957–59.* 10, No. 11.

37. *Canadian Universities—Historical.* Ottawa: Canadian

Department of External Affairs, Information Division,
No. 58, April 16, 1951.

38. CAPEN, SAMUEL P. "College Efficiency and Standardization," *Association of American Colleges Bulletin*, 1 (1915), pp. 141–150.

39. CAPEN, SAMUEL P. "College 'Lists' and Surveys Published by the Bureau of Education," *School and Society*, 6 (July 14, 1917), pp. 35–41.

40. CAPEN, SAMUEL P. *The Management of Universities.* Buffalo: Foster and Stewart Publishing Corp., 1953.

41. CAPEN, SAMUEL P. "The Principles Which Should Govern Standards and Accrediting Practices," *Educational Record*, 12 (April 1931), pp. 93–103.

42. CAPEN, SAMUEL P. "Seven Devils in Exchange for One," *Coordination of Accrediting Activities*, American Council on Education Studies, Series 1, Vol. 3, No. 9. Washington: American Council on Education, 1939, pp. 5–17.

43. CAPEN, SAMUEL P. "Vital Educational Measures Applicable to Colleges," *Association of American Colleges Bulletin*, 18 (March 1932), pp. 45–53.

44. CARNEGIE FOUNDATION FOR THE ADVANCEMENT OF TEACHING. *Annual Report.* Published annually since 1906. New York: the Foundation.

45. CARR-SAUNDERS, A. M. *Professions—Their Organization and Place in Society.* Oxford: Clarendon Press, 1928.

46. CHAMBERS, M. M. "Conflicting Theories of Social Control of Higher Education," *Phi Delta Kappan*, 13 (April 1931), pp. 186–192.

47. CHURCHILL, G. B. "Attitude of the Massachusetts Legislature Toward Standards for Degree-giving Institutions," *Education*, 40 (March 1920), pp. 432–452.

48. CLAPP, MARGARET, Ed. *The Modern University.* Ithaca: Cornell University Press, 1950.

49. COMMAGER, HENRY S. *The American Mind—An Interpretation of American Thought and Character Since the 1880's.* New Haven: Yale University Press, 1950.
50. COMMITTEE ON EDUCATION AND LABOR. *Diploma Mills.* Report of Sub-Committee Hearings on January 19, March 6, 19, and 28, 1924. United States Senate.
51. CONANT, JAMES B. *The Educational Stream Which Makes Possible the Professions.* Speech before Associated Harvard Clubs, Chicago, Illinois, May 20, 1938.
52. "CONFERENCE ON METHODS OF COLLEGE STANDARDIZATION," *Educational Record,* 2 (July 1921), pp. 81–122.
53. COOK, WALTER W. "Improvement of Legal Education and of Standards for Admission to the Bar," *American Law School Review,* 4 (December 1917), pp. 338–345.
54. *Cooperation and Coordination in Higher Education.* American Council on Education Studies, Series 1, Vol. 2, No. 5. Washington: American Council on Education, 1938.
55. *Cooperation in Accrediting Procedures.* American Council on Education Studies, Series 1, Vol. 5, No. 14. Washington: American Council on Education, 1941.
56. *Coordination of Accrediting Activities.* American Council on Education Studies, Series 1, Vol. 3, No. 9. Washington: American Council on Education, 1939.
57. COUNCIL OF STATE GOVERNMENTS. *Higher Education in the Forty-Eight States: A Report to the Governor's Conference.* Chicago: the Council, 1952.
58. COUNCIL ON COOPERATION IN TEACHER EDUCATION. *Desirable Policies for the Certification of Teachers.* Washington: American Council on Education, 1957.
59. COWLEY, W. H. "The American System of Academic Government," *Western College Association Proceedings,* November 1955, pp. 25–33.

60. COWLEY, W. H. "College and University Teaching, 1858–1958," *Educational Record,* 39 (October 1958), pp. 311–326.

61. COWLEY, W. H. "European Influences upon American Higher Education," *Educational Record,* 20 (April 1939), pp. 165–190.

62. COWLEY, W. H. "The Government and Administration of Higher Education: Whence and Whither," *Journal of the American Association of Collegiate Registrars,* 22 (July 1947), pp. 483–491.

63. COWLEY, W. H. "Professional Growth and Academic Freedom," *Western College Association Proceedings,* 1950, pp. 34–45.

64. COWLEY, W. H. "The University in the United States of America," in Edward Bradby, Ed., *The University Outside Europe.* London: Oxford University Press, 1939.

65. CRAMER, J. F., and BROWNE, G. S. *Contemporary Education—A Comparative Study of National Systems.* New York: Harcourt Brace & Co., 1956.

66. *Credit Given by Educational Institutions.* American Association of Collegiate Registrars and Admissions Officers. Published annually.

67. DAVIS, CALVIN O. *A History of the North Central Association of Colleges and Secondary Schools, 1895–1945.* Ann Arbor: the Association, 1945.

68. DEFERRARI, ROY J. *Self-Evaluation and Accreditation in Higher Education.* Washington: The Catholic University of America Press, 1959.

69. DODDS, HAROLD W. "Relation of Federal Government to Higher Education," *Association of American Universities Proceedings,* 1939, pp. 85–92.

70. DONALDSON, B. E. "Role of College Accreditation,"

Association of American Colleges Bulletin, 39 (May 1953), pp. 274–281.

71. DONOVAN, GEORGE F. *Developments in the Accreditation of Teacher Education in the United States.* Special Study No. 1. Washington: National Catholic Educational Association, September 1956.

72. DUFFUS, R. L. *Democracy Enters College.* New York: Charles Scribner's Sons, 1936.

73. EATON, JOHN. *Annual Report of the Commissioner.* U. S. Bureau of Education, 1873.

74. EDMONSON, J. B. "Responsibility for Diploma Mills," *Higher Education,* 10 (January 1954), pp. 88–89.

75. EDWARDS, MARCIA. "Products and Byproducts of Accreditation," *School and Society,* 47 (1938), pp. 90–94.

76. EDWARDS, MARCIA. *Studies on American Graduate Education.* New York: Carnegie Foundation for the Advancement of Teaching, 1944.

77. EELLS, WALTER CROSBY. *Surveys of American Higher Education.* New York: Carnegie Foundation for the Advancement of Teaching, 1937.

78. ELLIS, J. T. "Accreditation and the Catholic College," *Catholic Educational Review,* 34 (December 1936), pp. 589–597.

79. FARRAND, MAX. *The Framing of the Constitution of the U.S.* New Haven: Yale University Press, 1913.

80. FISHBEIN, MORRIS. "The Function and Future of the American Medical Association in Medical Education," *American Medical Association Journal,* 94 (March 29, 1930), pp. 911–915.

81. FLEXNER, ABRAHAM. *Medical Education in the United*

States and Canada. Boston: D. B. Updyke, Merry-
mount Press, 1910.

82. FRILEY, C. E. "Conflicting Aspects of Accrediting Procedures," *Association of Urban Universities Proceedings*, 1940, pp. 12–17.

83. FRILEY, C. E. "National Trends in Accrediting," *College
and University*, 25 (July 1950), pp. 539–547.

84. FUESS, CLAUDE M. *The College Board, Its First Fifty
Years.* New York: Columbia University Press, 1950.

85. GARBER, L. O., and CASTETTER, W. B. "Functions of
Government in Educational Control," *Annals of
American Academy of Political Science*, 265 (Septem-
ber 1949), pp. 25–34.

86. GARDNER, D. *The Evaluation of Higher Institutions,
Vol. 5, Student Personnel Services.* Chicago: University of Chicago Press, 1936.

87. GRINNELL, J. E. "The Rise of the North Central Association," *North Central Association Quarterly*, 9
(April 1935), pp. 468–495; also, 10 (1936) pp. 364–
382 and 469–526.

88. GUSTAVSON, R. G. "An Introduction and a History of
the Relationship of University and College Organizations to Accrediting Agencies," *Excerpts from
Addresses.* Washington: National Commission on
Accrediting, January 8, 1952.

89. GUSTAVSON, R. G. "Joint Committee on Accreditment,"
Association of American Colleges Bulletin, 35 (March
1949), pp. 50–55.

90. HACKER, LOUIS M. "Plight of Professors During the
'Difficult Years,'" *Saturday Review*, November 29,
1958, pp. 19–20.

91. HAGEN, O. J. "The Concept of Regionalism in Higher

Education," *Educational Record*, 18 (April 1937), pp. 147–158.

92. HAGGERTY, MELVIN E. *The Evaluation of Higher Institutions, Volume 3: The Educational Program*. Chicago: University of Chicago Press, 1936.

93. HAGGERTY, MELVIN E. *The Evaluation of Higher Institutions, Volume 2: The Faculty*. Chicago: University of Chicago Press, 1936.

94. HAGGERTY, MELVIN E. "The Product of Higher Educational Institutions," *North Central Association Quarterly*, 8 (September 1933), pp. 248–261.

95. HANSEN, ALLEN OSCAR. *Liberalism and American Education in the 18th Century*. New York: The Macmillan Co., 1926.

96. HARRIS, W. T. *Annual Report of the Commissioner*. U. S. Bureau of Education, 1888–1889; 1891–1892; 1895–1896; also, 1897–1898.

97. HASKINS, C. H. *The Rise of Universities*. New York: Henry Holt & Co., 1923.

98. HAZEN, H. L. "Relations with Regional Accrediting Associations," *Journal of Engineering Education*, 45 (November 1954), pp. 209–213.

99. HENDERSON, JOSEPH L. *Admission to College by Certificate*. New York: Columbia University Teachers College, 1912.

100. HENRY, DAVID D. "Suggestions from Beyond the Campus," *Excerpts from Addresses*. Washington: National Commission on Accrediting, January 8, 1952.

101. HERVEY, JOHN G. "The Decline of Professionalism in the Law: An Exploration into Some Causes," *New York Law Forum*, 3, No. 4 (October 1957).

102. "HIGHER EDUCATION IN THE SOUTH," *Southern Association Quarterly*, 11 (August 1947), pp. 472–640.

103. HILL, A. T. "What is a Nonaccredited College?" *Educational Record,* 38 (October 1957), pp. 348–354.

104. HILL, D. S. *Control of Tax-Supported Higher Education in the United States.* New York: Carnegie Foundation for the Advancement of Teaching, 1934.

105. HOFSTADTER, RICHARD, and HARDY, C. DeWITT. *Development and Scope of Higher Education in the United States.* New York: Columbia University Press, 1952.

106. HOLLIS, E. V. "Comprehensive Qualitative Accrediting," *Educational Record,* 21 (October 1940), pp. 506–537.

107. HOLMES, K. L. "Fixing Standards in Higher Education," *School and Society,* 27 (March 31, 1928), pp. 395–396.

108. HOOK, SIDNEY. "Education and Creative Intelligence," *School and Society,* 84 (July 7, 1956), pp. 3–8.

109. HORNER, H. H. *Education in New York State—1784–1954.* Albany: State Education Department, 1954.

110. HORNER, H. H. *The State and Higher Education.* Albany: University of the State of New York, 1939.

111. HUGHES, J. H. "Movement for the Accrediting of Liberal Arts Colleges," *American Association of Collegiate Registrars Journal,* 21 (January 1946), pp. 190–204.

112. HUNT, CHARLES W. "The Development of Standards in the Teachers Colleges," *Educational Administration and Supervision,* 19 (January 1933), pp. 11–17.

113. HUXLEY, JULIAN. "Are There Too Many of Us?" *Readers Digest,* 73 (December 1958), pp. 62–64.

114. JACOBSON, PAUL B. *Use of Tests by Accrediting Agencies in New Directions for Measurment and Guidance.* Washington: American Council on Education, Com-

mittee on Measurement and Guidance, Ser. 1, No. 20, Vol. 8 (August 1944), pp. 35–48.

115. JAMRICH, JOHN X. "Evaluation in College Teaching and Administration," *North Central Association Quarterly*, 33 (April 1959), pp. 288–293.

116. JESSUP, W. A. "Standardization and Achievement," *North Central Association Quarterly*, 7 (December 1932), pp. 265–269.

117. JOHNSON, VICTOR. "A History of the Council on Medical Education and Hospitals of the American Medical Association," in Morris Fishbein, Ed., *A History of the American Medical Associaton, 1847–1947*. Philadelphia: W. B. Saunders, 1947.

118. KELLY, FRED J. "Large Scale Planning in Higher Education," *North Central Association Quarterly*, 7 (March 1933), pp. 388–393.

119. KELLY, FRED J. "A Study of Recent Standardizing Activities of Certain Assocations Affecting University Organization and Curricula," *National Association of State Universities Proceedings*, 1926, Part 2.

120. KELLY, FRED J., and CAPEN, SAMUEL P. *The Influence of the Standardizing Agencies in Education*. Minneapolis: University of Minnesota, 1928.

121. KELLY, FRED J., FRAZIER, B. W., McNEELEY, JOHN H., and RATCLIFFE, ELLA B. *College Accreditation by Agencies Within States*. Bulletin 1940, No. 3. Washington: U. S. Office of Education, 1940.

122. KIRKPATRICK, J. E. *The American College and Its Rulers*. New York: New Republic, 1926.

123. KNIGHT, G. W. "The State and the Private College," *Educational Review*, 10 (June 1895), pp. 57–70.

124. LEWIS, ROY, and MAUDE, ANGUS. *Professional People*. London: Phoenix House, 1952.

125. LIEBERMAN, MYRON. *Education as a Profession.* Englewood Cliffs, New Jersey: Prentice-Hall, Inc., 1956.

126. LIMBERT, PAUL M. *Denominational Policies in the Support of Higher Education.* New York: Columbia University Teachers College, 1929.

127. LIPMAN, CHARLES B. "Profession Associations and Associations of Professional Schools and Some Problems Which They Pose for American Universities," *Association of American Universities Proceedings,* 1936, pp. 131–139.

128. MACLEAN, G. E. "An American Federation of Learning," *North Central Association of Colleges and Secondary Schools Proceedings,* 1906, pp. 3–25.

129. MACLEAN, G. E. *Present Standards of Higher Education in the U. S.* Bulletin 1913, No. 4. Washington: U. S. Bureau of Education, 1913.

130. MARVIN, C. H. "National Commission on Accrediting," *Association of American Colleges Bulletin,* 36 (March 1950), pp. 53–64.

131. McCONN, C. M. "Academic Standards versus Individual Differences—the Dilemma of Democratic Education," *American School Board Journal,* 91 (December 1935), p. 44.

132. McHALE, KATHRYN. "Search for Values Through Accrediting Agencies," *Association of American Colleges Bulletin,* 20 (March 1934), pp. 125–131.

133. McKEAN, DAYTON D. "Who's in Charge Here? The Universities or the Professional Associations?" *The Colorado Quarterly,* 6 (Spring 1958), pp. 395–408.

134. McNEELY, JOHN H. *Supervision Exercised by States over Privately Controlled Institutions of Higher Education.* Bulletin 1934, No. 8. Washington: U. S. Office of Education, 1934.

135. McVey, W. E. "Developing Accreditation Standards," *Phi Delta Kappan*, 27 (May 1946), pp. 253–256.

136. Middle States Association of Colleges and Secondary Schools. *Proceedings*. Published annually since 1887.

137. Millett, John D. *Financing Higher Education in the United States*. New York: Columbia University Press, 1952.

138. Millis, John S. "Major Purposes of Accrediting," *Report of Workshop Conference on Accreditation, June 1957*. Washington: National Commission on Accrediting, 1957.

139. Moncure, J. C. "Accrediting Conference of the American Council on Education," *Journal of the American Association of University Women*, 32 (June 1939), pp. 240–242.

140. Monroe, Walter S., Ed. *Encyclopedia of Educational Research*. New York: The Macmillan Co., 1950.

141. National Association of State Universities. *Proceedings*. Published annually since 1903.

142. National Commission on Accrediting. "Minutes of Commission and of Executive Committee Meetings." Annually since 1949.

143. National Commission on Accrediting. *Statement of Criteria for Recognized Accrediting Agencies*. Washington: the Commission, March 2, 1957.

144. National Committee of Regional Accrediting Agencies. "General Principles for the Establishment of Comprehensive Evaluation Procedures by a Regional Accrediting Association," adopted by the Committee, October 25, 1952. *Northwest Association of Secondary and Higher Schools Proceedings*, 1952.

145. NATIONAL CONFERENCE COMMITTEE ON STANDARDS OF COLLEGES AND SECONDARY SCHOOLS. *Minutes of Annual Conferences.* Middletown, Connecticut: Press of Pelton and King, 1906–1921.

146. NEVINS, JOHN F. *A Study of the Organization and Operation of Voluntary Accrediting Agencies.* Washington: The Catholic University of America Press, 1959.

147. NEWBURN, HARRY K. "Extension of the Accrediting Function of Regional Associations," *Northwest Association of Secondary and Higher Schools Proceedings,* 1950, pp. 53–61; also, *Association of American Colleges Bulletin,* 37 (December 1951), pp. 472–482.

148. NEWBURN, HARRY K. "The Organization and Administration of Universities in France, Italy and Great Britain," *Educational Record,* 34 (July 1953), pp. 245–274.

149. NEW ENGLAND ASSOCIATION OF COLLEGES AND SECONDARY SCHOOLS. *Introducing the New England Association.* Boston: the Association, undated.

150. NEW ENGLAND ASSOCIATION OF COLLEGES AND SECONDARY SCHOOLS. *New England Association Review.* Published irregularly since 1952.

151. NEW ENGLAND ASSOCIATION OF COLLEGES AND SECONDARY SCHOOLS. *Proceedings.* Published intermittently 1885 to 1908.

152. NEWLON, JESS H. "How Can Standardizing Agencies Best Serve the Course of Education in the Future?" *North Central Association Quarterly,* 3 (September 1929), pp. 208–213.

153. NEWMAN, ROBERT P. "British Higher Education," *The Thirty-second Discussion and Debate Manual, 1 (1958–59),* pp. 173–186. Columbia, Missouri: Lucas Brothers Publishers.

154. NICHOLSON, FRANK W. "The Certificate System in New England," *Educational Review,* 42 (December 1911), pp. 486–503.

155. NORTH CENTRAL ASSOCIATION OF COLLEGES AND SECONDARY SCHOOLS. *Proceedings.* Published annually 1896–1925.

156. NORTH CENTRAL ASSOCIATION OF COLLEGES AND SECONDARY SCHOOLS. "Proposed New Basis for the Accrediting of Higher Institutions," *North Central Association Quarterly,* 8 (April 1934), pp. 419–424.

157. *North Central Association Quarterly.* North Central Association of Colleges and Secondary Schools. Published quarterly since 1926.

158. NORTHWEST ASSOCIATION OF SECONDARY AND HIGHER SCHOOLS. *Proceedings.* Published annually since 1918.

159. NOYES, W. A., JR. "The Program of the Committee on the Professional Training of Chemists," *Association of American Universities Proceedings,* 1945, pp. 80–85.

160. NYQUIST, EWALD B. "National and Regional Developments in Cooperative Evaluation and Accrediting Activity," *Journal of Engineering Education,* 44 (May 1954), pp. 533–538.

161. OBOLER, ELI M. *College and University Library Accreditation Standards 1957,* Monograph 20. Chicago: Association of College and Research Libraries, 1958.

162. PATTILLO, MANNING M. "Accrediting in the Public Interest," *Educational Record,* 36 (April 1955), pp. 120–128.

163. PATTILLO, MANNING M. "Recent Developments in Accrediting," *North Central Association Quarterly,* 27 (January 1953), pp. 290–292.

164. PENCHE, WILLIAM L. "Degrees for Sale," *National*

Education Association Journal, 38 (December 1945), pp. 286–287.

165. PERRY, R. C. "Trends in the Accreditation of Post-Secondary Institutions," *American Association of Collegiate Registrars Journal,* 7 (January 1942), pp. 210–225.

166. PFNISTER, ALLAN O. "A Regional Accrediting Agency Experiments in the Training of Consultants for Higher Educational Institutions," *Educational Record,* 40 (January 1959), pp. 62–68.

167. PIERSON, G. W. "American Universities in the 19th Century: The Formative Period," in Margaret Clapp, Ed., *The Modern University.* Ithaca: Cornell University Press, 1950.

168. PIERSON, W. W. "Remarks of the President," *Southern University Conference Proceedings,* 1954, pp. 59–65.

169. PINCHOT, GIFFORD. "The State, the Nation and the People's Needs," *Annals of Academy of Political and Social Sciences,* 129 (January 1927), pp. 72–76.

170. PINKHAM, F. O. "The Accrediting Problem," *Annals of American Academy of Political Science,* 103 (September 1955), pp. 67–71.

171. PINKHAM, F. O. "The National Commission on Accrediting Progress Report," *Northwest Association of Secondary and Higher Schools Proceedings,* December 1952.

172. POUND, ROSCOE. *The Lawyer from Antiquity to Modern Times.* St. Paul: West Publishing Company, 1953.

173. PRESIDENT'S COMMITTEE ON EDUCATION BEYOND THE HIGH SCHOOL. *Second Report to the President.* Washington: Government Printing Office, 1957.

174. PRITCHETT, HENRY S. "Sham Universities," *Annual Report of the Carnegie Foundation for the Advancement of Teaching,* 1912, pp. 154–163.

175. PRITCHETT, HENRY S. "Should the Carnegie Foundation Be Suppressed?" *North American Review*, 201 (April 1915), pp. 554–566.

176. PRITCHETT, HENRY S. "Standards and Standardizers," *School and Society*, 1 (March 6, 1915), pp. 336–339.

177. PULLIAS, E. V. "Some Special Responsibilities of Accrediting Agencies," *Educational Record*, 39 (October 1958), pp. 340–347.

178. RASHDALL, HASTINGS. *The Universities of Europe in the Middle Ages*. Powick, F. M., and Emden, A. B., Eds. 3 Vols. Oxford: The Clarendon Press, 1936.

179. REED, ALFRED Z. "Accrediting Agencies," *Annual Report of the Carnegie Foundation for the Advancement of Teaching*, 1939, pp. 29–44.

180. REED, ALFRED Z. "Contribution of the Medieval University to American Higher Education," *Annual Report of the Carnegie Foundation for the Advancement of Teaching*, 1936, pp. 52–69.

181. REED, ALFRED Z. "Learned Professions and Their Organization," *Annual Report of the Carnegie Foundation for the Advancement of Teaching*, 1933, pp. 63–89.

182. REED, ALFRED Z. "Origins of Licensing in the Learned Professions," *Annual Report of the Carnegie Foundation for the Advancement of Teaching*, 1938, pp. 68–86.

183. REEVES, F. W. "Need for New Methods of Accrediting Institutions of Higher Learning," *American Association of University Professors Bulletin*, 17 (November 1931), pp. 522–530.

184. REEVES, F. W. "New Standards of Institutional Evaluation," *American Association of Collegiate Registrars Proceedings*, 1933, pp. 307–319.

185. REEVES, F. W. "Standards for Accrediting Colleges," *American Association of Collegiate Registrars Proceedings*, July 1927, pp. 94–117.

186. REID, ROBERT H. *American Degree Mills*. Washington: American Council on Education, 1959 (in process of publication).

187. REINERT, PAUL C. "Present Status of Accreditation in Higher Education," *College and University*, 29 (July 1954), pp. 583–591.

188. REISNER, EDWARD H. "Antecedents of the Federal Acts Concerning Education," *Educational Record*, 11 (July 1930), pp. 196–207.

189. RIESMAN, DAVID. "Planning in Higher Education: Some Notes on Patterns and Problems." Talk at Symposium in Social Change, American Anthropological Association Annual Meeting, November 1958.

190. ROCKEFELLER BROTHERS FUND. *The Pursuit of Excellence—Education and the Future of America*. Special Studies Project, Report 5. New York: Doubleday and Co., 1958.

191. RUDOLPH, FREDERICK. *Mark Hopkins and the Log—Williams College: 1836–1872*. New Haven: Yale University Press, 1956.

192. RUSSELL, J. D. *The Outlook for Higher Education*. Chicago: University of Chicago Press, 1939.

193. RUSSELL, J. D., and JUDD, C. H. *The American Educational System*. Cambridge: The Riverside Press, 1940.

194. RUSSELL, J. D., and MACKENZIE, D. M., Eds. *Emergent Responsibilities in Higher Education*. Chicago: University of Chicago Press, 1946.

195. RUSSELL, J. D., and REEVES, F. W. *The Evaluation of Higher Institutions, Volume 6: Administration*. Chicago: University of Chicago Press, 1936.

196. SAVAGE, HOWARD. "Carnegie Foundation and the Rise of the Unit," *Annual Report of the Carnegie Foundation for the Advancement of Teaching*, 1947–1948, pp. 13–30.

197. SELDEN, WILLIAM K. "Accrediting—What Is It?" *American Association of University Professors Bulletin*, 42 (December 1956), pp. 629–635.

198. SELDEN, WILLIAM K. "National Commission on Accrediting; Its Next Mission," *Educational Record*, 38 (April 1957), pp. 152–156.

199. SILLS, K. C. M. "Report of Committee on Standards for Colleges: Institutions in New England Which Grant Degrees," *Education*, 46 (March 1926), pp. 428–434.

200. SMITH, W. O. LESTER. *Education—An Introductory Survey*. New York: Penguin Books, 1957.

201. SNAVELY, GUY E. "A Short History of the Southern Association of Colleges and Secondary Schools," *Southern Association Quarterly*, 9 (November 1945), pp. 423–549.

202. SOUTHERN ASSOCIATION OF COLLEGES AND SECONDARY SCHOOLS. *Proceedings*. Published annually commencing 1895.

203. *Southern Association Quarterly*. Southern Association of Colleges and Secondary Schools. Published quarterly 1937–1947.

204. SPURLOCK, CLARK. *Education and the Supreme Court*. Urbana: University of Illinois Press, 1955.

205. STORR, RICHARD J. *The Beginnings of Graduate Education in America*. Chicago: University of Chicago Press, 1953.

206. STUIT, D. B., HELMSTADTER, G. C., and FREDERICKSEN, N. *Survey of College Evaluation Methods and Needs: A Report to the Carnegie Corporation*. Princeton,

New Jersey: Educational Testing Service, December 1956.

207. TALBOT, MARION, and ROSENBERRY, LOUIS K. M. *The History of the American Association of University Women*. Cambridge: Houghton Mifflin Co., 1931.
208. TEWKSBURY, DONALD. *Founding of Colleges and Universities Before the Civil War*. New York: Columbia University Teachers College, 1932.
209. THWING, CHARLES F. *A History of Higher Education in America*. New York: D. Appleton & Co., 1906.
210. TIGERT, JOHN J., "Objectionable Practices of Accrediting Agencies," *School and Society*, 50 (September 23, 1939), pp. 407–410.
211. TOURTELLOT, ARTHUR B. *The General Recognition of Accountancy as a Profession*. New York: American Institute of Accountants, 1956.
212. TRYON, RUTH W. *The AAUW—1881–1949*. Washington: American Association of University Women, 1950.
213. TURBEVILLE, G. "How We Got Accredited," *Association of American Colleges Bulletin*, 43 (October 1957), pp. 428–434.

214. UNITED STATES OFFICE OF EDUCATION. "Criteria for Determining Nationally Recognized Accrediting Agencies and Associations," *Higher Education*, 9 (November 1952), p. 70.

215. WAPLES, DOUGLAS. *The Evaluation of Higher Institutions, Vol. 4: The Library*. Chicago: University of Chicago Press, 1936.
216. WARD, BARBARA. "Economic NATO for One Billion," *New York Times Magazine*, October 19, 1958.
217. WESLEY, EDGAR B. *NEA—The First 100 Years—The*

Building of the Teaching Profession. New York: Harper & Brothers, 1957.

218. WHITE, ANDREW D. *Some Important Questions in Higher Education.* Ithaca, New York: Andrus and Church, 1885.

219. WHITNEY, A. S. "Methods in Use of Accrediting Schools," *Middle States Association of Colleges and Secondary Schools Proceedings,* 1902, pp. 20–30.

220. WILBUR, R. L. "Maintaining Standards Without Excessive Standardization," *Association of American Universities Proceedings,* 1924, pp. 59–65.

221. WILKINS, THERESA B. *Accredited Higher Institutions 1956,* Bulletin 1957, No. 1 Washington: U. S. Office of Education, 1957.

222. WILSON, WOODROW. "School and College," *Middle States Association of Colleges and Secondary Schools Proceedings,* 1907, pp. 73–89.

223. WINSHIP, ALBERT E. "Standardization—Wise and Otherwise," *National Education Association Proceedings,* 1915, pp. 528–533.

224. WITMER, S. A. "An Evaluation of Professional Accrediting Agencies." Ph.D. dissertation, University of Chicago, 1951.

225. WRISTON, HENRY M. "New Procedures of Accrediting Recently Adopted by the North Central Association," *American Association of University Professors Bulletin* 21 (March 1935), pp. 206–210.

226. WRISTON, HENRY M. "The Search for Values Through Accreditation," *Association of American Colleges Bulletin,* 20 (March 1934), pp. 98–131.

227. ZOOK, GEORGE F. "Accrediting of Higher Institutions," *School and Society,* 43 (April 25, 1936), pp. 553–562.

228. ZOOK, GEORGE F. "The Bureau of Education and Higher Education," *School Life*, 9 (May 1924), pp. 199–201.

229. ZOOK, GEORGE F. "The Incorporation and Accrediting of Universities and Colleges," *American Association of Collegiate Registrars Proceedings*, 2 (July 1926), pp. 110–123.

230. ZOOK, GEORGE F. "President's Annual Report," *Educational Record*, 20 (July 1939), p. 359; 30 (July 1949), pp. 275–280; also, 31 (July 1950), pp. 247–250.

231. ZOOK, GEORGE F. "Who Should Control our Higher Institutions?" *Association of Land-Grant Colleges and Universities Proceedings*, 1938, pp. 90–99; also, *Educational Record*, 20 (January 1939), pp. 28–43.

232. ZOOK, GEORGE F., and HAGGERTY, MELVIN E. *The Evaluation of Higher Institutions, Vol. 1: Principles of Accrediting Higher Institutions*. Chicago: University of Chicago Press, 1936.

Index

133